SELF-EMP1

177 Lucrative Businesses You Can Start Without Money

177Ways to Create Your Own Jobs without Money, Office, Tools, Expensive Equipment, or Pay Any Bills.

By Ucheka Anofienem

First Published in Nigeria, January, 2017 by

Skill Development Information System Ltd

177 Lucrative Businesses You Can Start Without Money

Copyright © 2016 by Ucheka Anofienem

All rights reserved. No part of this publication may be reproduced, stored in a retrieval system, or transmitted in any form or by any means, electronic, mechanical, photocopying, recording or otherwise, without prior permission in writing from the publisher.

Ucheka Anofienem

Ucheka is an information entrepreneur, business idea, and concept development expert, an author of too many best-selling business and self-help books. He is a director with Skill Development Information System Ltd.

Contacts:

Skill Development Information System Ltd

Preferred Books, 46B Mug Plaza, Opposite (Mug Plaza) Area 7, Garki, Abuja, Nigeria.

Email: ucheka1968@gmail.com

Social Media Platforms:

https://twitter.com@uchekaa

https://www.facebook.com@ucheka.anofienem

https://ng.linkedin.com/in@ucheka-anofienem-75638435

https://www.goodreads.com/user/show/16329887-ucheka-anofienem

Tel: 234(0)8164746117

Table of Contents

BUSINESSES YOU CAN START WITHOUT MONEY (OR LITTLE OF IT)   8

Number One: Home Service Businesses   8

Number Two: Marketing, Sales and Public Relation Services   17

Number Three: Internet and Online Businesses that Can Earn You Money   30

Number Four: Events Planning and Promotion   36

Number Five: Office and Personal Services   39

Number Six: Editorial Services   44

Number Seven: Simple Agro Related Ventures   46

Number Eight: Jewelry and Artwork Business   50

Number Nine: Exercise and Fitness Business   52

Number Ten: Personalized Services   54

Number Eleven: Modern Ways to Make Money Easily   57

ENTREPRENEURIAL AND SELF-EMPLOYMENT SKILLS TO OUTSELL COMPETITORS   66

It will help if you are familiar with the following fundamental facts: 66

UNDERSTANDING WHY SMALL BUSINESSES FAIL 76

CHAPTER 4: 84

50 IDEAS THAT GIVE YOU HUGE ADVANTAGE AS A BUSINESS OWNER 84

Foreword

Most people are unemployed because they are unwilling to take actions on what they already know that can earn them money. Information, knowledge or awareness is not the challenge, the real trouble is in getting people to decide with absolute commitment to make effort and create their own jobs.

This book answers two basic questions for the readers. First, it itemizes those businesses that anybody can start with little or no money, requiring no equipment, tool, office, or need to pay any bill. Second, it explains the steps that guarantee success for anyone who desires to act on those business ideas identified. One of the most priced assets is the ability to take self-help business initiative to get out of poor conditions.

The truth is, government cannot afford to give jobs to all the millions of unemployed people neither can it facilitate funding for everyone to start their businesses. The best help people can find lies in their own hands and in their own minds. It all depends on them to really put their minds to work and take decisive steps in creating their own employment, and this book has already done most of the thinking and laid bare the action plans.

People are unaware that a simple initiative that requires no special skill can put lots of money in their hands almost immediately. It is all about figuring out how to be sensitive to needs, challenges and desires of people, and then provide creative solution to those needs. This book is about knowing how to profit by providing values to people, leveraging from every day and newly emerging opportunities that are commonly neglected.

Information is a powerful liberator from ignorance and sufferings only if acted upon. This work gives you all the ideas that will put you on the job, working for yourself and making all the money you can the very hour you put it down. This happens only if you take action to apply the knowledge gained. An unemployed person can easily make more money selling products or services (his own or other people's products or services) than looking to get a salaried job in a crowded job market such as ours. It is much easier getting people to buy the things you sell than getting employed into a vacancy that a thousand other folks are equally interested in.

There are lots of Internet and online businesses thrown up daily from which people are making money legitimately. The reality is that the internet has changed the way business is done and it is the economy of the millennium. Anyone ignorant about how to key in and take lucrative advantage of it to make money or promote his business is undoing himself. People should deplore their creativity into simple things that generate money. Innovative ideas that provide solutions are always welcomed. Hard times provide the best opportunity for people to be inventive in creating opportunities. It does not always take money to do this. Once you start, support will come to you.

Think mainly of service products, intangible items and especially non-physical services rather than physical products that will require finances and other logistics to execute. You have an idea, and you know how to sell the idea to a potential customer, collect his money, get the materials, deliver or install it, and then keep the profit. No matter the ideas you encounter in this book, it is you that will bring the creativity that will make it work, and that creativity is here for you.

Pay attention to those marketing information at the end of the book that shows you how to leverage on other people's skills, other people's money, other people's equipment, offices, contacts, and resources that you do not have. You leverage these possibilities by creatively bringing in advantage that can motivate these people with advantages you don't have to cooperate with you to achieve your objective of making money.

Finally, any self-driven person that reads this book and resolves to apply the ideas contained have my assurance that he will be a success story in the shortest possible time. I strongly recommend that all unemployed and underemployed folks should get this book and thoroughly digest every word in it. It gives joy and freedom to work for oneself!

Ucheka Anofienem

Chapter 1

Businesses You Can Start without Money (or little of it)
Number One: Home Service Businesses

#1. Run Mobile Kitchen. If you can cook varieties of food very well, then target rich people who are busy. You will not only prepare what they will need for the whole week, they will call you when they want to host their friends, organize birthday parties for their children, or celebrate anything. Go to their homes, collect their money, go to the market buy things and cook right there in their residence. They like it better when they see you do it. If they are satisfied they will introduce you to their friends as well. Impress them and they can pay in tens of thousands for a day's job. They will call you every week. Acquire plenty of such customers and you are in business.

#2. Healthcare Restaurant for Families with Health Challenges. Learn to prepare special diet (food and drinks) for people with health problems and you will always get calls. Target people who are watching their diet but have no correct knowledge of what it means to eat healthy. Many people in average and rich families suffer from obesity, weight concerns, cancer, diabetics, high blood pressure, ulcer, and they require special food diets.

Remember, many of them are ignorant and do not know that what they are eating is what is killing them. Prove to them that you understand the meals that will make them healthy. They will gladly engage and pay you. Health care restaurant is creative and new, talk to people directly to provide what they need as you do not have to open a restaurant for it. Go into it- learn to juice the fruits, blend the vegetables, bake and toast without fats, oil and sugar. Announce yourself, print the flyers and share, then watch as calls will start coming.

#3. Baby-Sit for Working Mothers. Daycare, nanny or crèche business is popular, and you can always start and then take steps to get the necessary approvals, depending on where you live. You can use your residence to start. Approach affluent nursing mothers in your neighborhood. There are single mothers who work and will need someone to take care of their babies while they are away. Talk to single working-class mothers wherever you can find them. It maybe they are not satisfied with the person or place they are using at the moment. Show them the place you want to use for it. Beg them to try out with you.

If possible, reduce the charges for a start. If they are satisfied with your services and the way you take care of their babies, they will not complain if you increase the fees. Make the environment very decent; employ additional hands if you have many children to attend to. You can get a place close to where there are lots of office. Publicize and directly talk with rich people and they will give you a trial. You recognize rich people who can pay by the type of cars they drive, or the kind of houses they live. Identify people who can pay good fee, go directly and talk to them.

#4. Nanny Placement. For busy parents, finding a good nanny isn't a child's play. Nanny placement agents who screen applicants, check references, match personalities, and set schedules- provide clients an invaluable service by saving them considerable time and worry. People are very careful and will not just want to dump their children without doing background check. They don't have the time to do that and you can fill that gap. They will pay you.

#5. Wash/Clean People's Car on the Spot. Go to busy estates, shopping plaza, banks premises, markets, business districts, block of flats, car park in office complexes, etc. Approach anybody who drives in with a dirty car/vehicle for permission to clean it up within five minutes. They will agree. With soap and water, you can clean up the car without water dropping on the ground. Employ other people, dress them up in uniform and concentrate on getting customers. You will make much money. There is no body doing this business. It's open!

#6. Special Services for Clients in Restaurant. Attach yourself to a restaurant and reach agreement to prepare special cultural foods that some categories of their customers will like- completely different from the usual menu list they serve. For example, your focus is only on Ghana food, Hausa food, or fresh fish pepper soup. They will agree for you to use their space and facilities to do your own business.

#7. Personal Chef. The difference with this is that people may want to engage you permanently. Those with culinary competence can likely find a hungry clientele among the rich busy working families. As stated above, target people who are on special diet, especially over weight, diabetic, cancer and ulcer patients. People who watch their diet and vegetarians usually need someone with knowledge of nutrition. Most rich people with health challenges watch what they eat and will be glad to engage someone devoted to managing their meals. Identify and approach them. There are waiting clients among the rich right now. Their wives have no time to go to the market, talk to them and you'll get their money.

#8. Personal Shopper. Help people do their shopping. In your street, give out your numbers. Busy mothers will always call you to rush down to markets and grocery stores to pick one item or the other. Believe this, you will never lack work to do if you can be trusted with money and safety.

#9. Children's Transportation Service- Pick their children to and from school. Make yourself useful to working parents who are always troubled with the idea of rushing out of important meetings to pick their kids from school. You will be engaged and of course, be paid handsomely.

#10. Window Washing. Check big churches, big office complexes, and shopping malls for business. Get the job and outsource

#11. Residential and Office Cleaning. It doesn't matter if the opportunity is already contracted to a company. You can approach them, offer cheaper charges and better-quality cleaning service. They can hire you to replace the other fellow. Start with cleaning windows, sweeping offices, toilet wash, etc. Then, as you accumulate money, you can buy the machines, and you can expand industrially into fumigation services.

Any business plaza with dirty corridors, untidy stairways and stinking toilets are great opportunities. Approach the management and they can give you the job instantly. Many government offices, civic institutions, schools, clinics, hospitals, company premises both inside and outside have a need for individuals who will provide cleaning services at a low cost outside of business hours. They are always looking for people who can work a few hours late at night, very early in the morning or on weekends. Approach them and propose to charge 30% less what their present contractor is being paid and they will consider you. you can always increase your price later.

#12. Landscaping Services. Approach compounds and housing estates with over grown flowers and bushy fences. You will be engaged to trim the wild flowers covering their fence. Be willing to mow lawns, clear bushes and cut tree branches? Many people are quite happy to pay for such services. By the time you go through your entire neighborhood, or areas where rich people reside you will get as many clients as you can manage. Look get the job and engage laborers to do it. You need not be the one clearing the bushes.

#13. House cleaning Services. Many people do not have the time, or simply don't enjoy cleaning their homes and are willing to pay a reasonable price to have someone do the work for them. Go round families where both couples are working full time. Many wives are scared and frustrated when they look at the heap of clothes they must wash, especially where they have children. Step in and help out. You will have lots of work to do and lots of money too.

14. Senior Citizen Assistance. Many elderly people need assistance with a wide variety of simple household tasks – cleaning, buying food stuff, laundry, cooking, and so forth. Many children of elderly people or retirees are quite willing to hire someone to help out their parents. Take an audit of elderly people who live alone and then ask to be of help and you will be surprised the kind of jobs you have on your hands.

#15. Gardening Services. The demand is out there. People have space at their backyard, but do not have the time to till the ground, plant the tomatoes and vegetables. Some people are willing to pay others to get a vegetable or flower garden started for them in their yard so they can have access to ultra-fresh produce without all the legwork or energy. Meet them and ask to serve in such capacities. They will oblige and pay you.

#16. Lawn Care. Approach people to be taking care of their compounds. They usually do not have time to tame the flowers, or cut the grass, they will be happy to let you do it for them. If you can do a good job mowing, clipping and fertilizing lawns for office complexes and residential clients, they are sure to introduce you to other people.

#17. Home-Entertainment Installation. Attach yourself to electronic dealers and simply follow their customer's home to help fix their new purchase. Novice get frustrated when they attempt to connect the wires, plugs, cables and other components of their new stereo and television sets. Step in with your sound electrical and wiring expertise, you'll have all systems working in no time. They will pay you for saving them from hassles.

#18. Home-Inspection Service. Work with estate agents and valuers. A keen eye for structural detail paves the way to success in your home-inspection service. Start by assessing clients' homes for problems such as structural damage and foundation abnormalities, then refer customers to contractors who can ensure their homes are in good repair. You will profit from both ends.

#19. Estate Agency. People are looking for houses to rent and do not have the time to do the searching by themselves. Fill in the gap for them. There are people who have properties to sell but do not know how to find buyers. Help them and you will be paid. A little research will tell you how to go about it. You can apprentice with someone who is into it and he will guide you.

#20. Carpet Washing and Dyeing. Hotels and most homes have unsightly or stained carpets. Carpet-dyeing professionals provide hotels, individuals, nursing homes and other businesses an attractive alternative. So go ahead, wash rugs for people in your neighborhood, lay the options at your clients' feet and they will give you the go ahead, and money will follow.

#21. Handyman Services. Do you have the skills to fix damaged stuffs? Advertise in local radio and newspapers, and soon you will be so busy with jobs, repairing everything from leaky pipes and stopped-up toilets, electrical faults, jammed cabinet drawers to broken windows. Just learn some technical skills that you can trade for money.

#22. Packing and Unpacking Service. Packing up to move to a new home or office is a lot of tiring job. Become a packing and unpacking entrepreneur. Find the client, rent the truck, get the boys to move the properties, and you are in business. Just let your community residents know you do such business and you could save many people time and lots of hassles. Leave your contact with estate agents so they can give to renters who will want to move immediately.

#23. Swimming Pool Services. Most mansions with swimming pools will be glad if you offer to give them or their family members swimming lessons. Make contact with home owners, recreation centres, apartment complexes and individual residences. People who have swimming pools will want their children to be taught how to swim before throwing themselves inside the water. Get the job, then get a trainer who can train them, collect the money, pay the guy and keep the balance. Always leverage on other people's skills.

#24. Home Decoration. Work with local furniture and accessory stores, paint shops, carpet and drapery outlets to coordinate clients' interiors. The key here is decorating your own home, first. From the good job done elsewhere, satisfied customers can always refer their friends to you. be bold to approach people and say to them, "Hello, I have special skills to decorate your home and it will have a special new look. Can I show you my catalogue?" Go online and make a download and compile specially decorated homes. Make an album of this and people will be instantly attracted. Get their money to buy the flower, wall paper, paint to do the work, or give to the person who can do it. You don't need to have the skills to do business. Get the job and outsource.

#25. Domestic Employee Services. Many school leavers are looking for work to do as domestic workers, shop attendants, and baby sitters. Employ them, train them, then go to big banks, government ministries, agencies, multinational, international NGOs, embassies, and other rich establishments and publicize. Also advertise in local radio programs. You will get calls when your packaging is mature and attractive. You can start before you register it. Develop and make it decent. Deal with only mature applicants and not little children.

You can as well recruit drivers for private persons and companies. Do good documentation, due diligence check to verify the reliability of the person you are employing. You can recruit security staff for small companies and private homes that do not want to deal with the big companies. Help busy parents babysit so they can go have fun. They'll pay.

#26. Laundry Services. Go from house to house in your neighborhood and collect clothes including bed sheets, blankets, rugs and any things you can handle. They will give. Meet people that glory in the kind of shirt they wear and ask them to give you their clothes to wash for them. All you have to do is to employ one person to assist you. You need just pressing iron, table, blanket and an electric connection. Beg people if possible and they will patronize you. Be serious and handle the one given to you very well, more will come and you will be in business for money. Go to people's home to collect their clothes, don't wait for them to bring it to you.

#27. Graffiti Removal & Abatement. Anywhere you see such desecrating inscriptions on toilet walls, fence walls, corridors, etc. go ask for permission to remove them. Schools, city centres, and commercial building owners will engage you.

#28. Coaching Services. Can you develop expertise in any special skills and teach it to people? Say for example, you go online and learn about special diet foods and drinks for diabetic and high pretension patients. Then you use social media platforms to market your services of teaching these skills to mothers and women so they serve their family. Do you believe you can get call? If you record this information in tapes, podcast, DVDs, YouTube, etc. people will buy and subscribe, and you can develop coaching program on this and sell and make money. Coaching opportunities abound, the question is what do you have to teach others? Answer this question and you will be on job.

Number Two: Marketing, Sales and Public Relation Services

#1. Show Companies Opportunities They Have to Make Money But Are Not Taking Advantage of. Find out opportunities that exist in companies that can make them money that they are not aware of or are not taking advantage of at the moment. Do they have seminar or conference halls that can be converted to commercial use? Have you observed the way they do business and can give suggestions to reduce their expense? Is their building strategic and good for outdoor advertising (billboard) placement? Can their skilled staff take up consultancy services at the same time to make more money for the company? Can they rent their office equipment and machines to make more money without disrupting their own operations?

Look at suggestions you can give a company that will enable them to make more money. Send them a proposal to that effect and they will call you. Negotiate the percentage they will pay you if your ideas make money for them. Do not give details until you have reached a firm agreement regarding payment. Believe it, you will make money when you make this your business.

#2. Place Adverts in Airlines and Bus Tickets. Negotiate with airline or transport company to brand their tickets with adverts from big companies. Get their permission, get the big companies to place the adverts, use the money collected from the companies to print and distribute the ticket to their offices. You will make money.

#3. Get Exclusive Right to Commercialize Big Public Events. In big seminars and conference, conventions, negotiate with organizers for the exclusive right to sale and advertisements. (Companies can place banners at the podium), book selling, food vendor and all merchandize in the venue will be under your control. They will oblige, then all people intending to do business at the venue will register, pay and obtain permission through you. You collect the money, pay the organizers and retain the balance. That's a good idea that nobody is thinking about. Negotiate with churches that organize frequent conventions, or crusade. Enter agreement with event centres, seminar organizers, training consultants, etc. Just any crowd puling event that will cause traders to congregate and start selling their articles is an opportunity for you to initiate a deal with the organizers.

#4. Partner with Building Contractors and Developers. If you know a contractor handling big project like estate complex, office or residential block, negotiate with him to refer all intending material suppliers and subcontractors to register with the company through you. Or, reach an agreement with the company to be the only one to source for all the materials for the project (suppliers and subcontractors will lobby you), then agree with them on the percentage to pay you for allowing them to supply cement, iron rods, roofing, etc. Just negotiate it; it is possible the company will agree and both of you will make money in the process.

#5. Media Advert Agent. Collect advertisements for newspapers, radios, and televisions. They will produce the jingles and pay your commission. Liaise with journalists at press centers and they will be glad to help you. Look at upcoming birthdays, or public awards of VIPs that will necessitate congratulatory messages. Target politicians, business moguls and public office holders and think of their friends that may like to place adverts in the media and contact them. Be proactive and approach people. The commission they pay is attractive if you can be committed to it.

#6. Placing Advert on Cars. Negotiate with companies to get them buses (especially long busses) and taxis on which you can place their mobile adverts. Take their money, get the vehicle owners and pay them to carry the adverts. If the vehicles commute on town services or long-distance travels on busy routes where a lot of potential customers would see that advert, then you've got a good argument to market to your prospective client. Try this out. Get the right from transporters and companies will come to you. The back of tricycles, the roof of taxis, the both sides of long and short busses are good advert spaces. Even parcel delivery bikes brand the message boxes with advert from other companies. Have you seen that?

#7. Be a Printing Agent. Go round and collect printing jobs from companies and people who want to print calendars, almanacs, greeting cards, diaries, complimentary cards, identity cards, etc. When you publicize yourself as a publisher, many people who have written books or pamphlets will patronize you. Visit churches and ask if they want to print flyers. Leave your contact and they will call you any time they have need for it.

Whenever you collect a job deliver promptly as you have promised. Do not play pranks after you have collected money from people. Use experienced graphic designers and sit down with them to do the work, print out in film and take to lithographers to lay in plates, take it to the printing machine, buy rim of papers and give them to run the impression, take to finishers for collation, stitching (or hot binding) and trimming. Collect your finished job and deliver to your client. You make profit this way rather than handing the job over to another printing contractor.

#8. Set Up Hundreds of Joint Venture Deals by Making Series of Initiatives. For example, if you cannot write books, get someone who can write to develop documents that will be useful to school children and teachers, and take it to state governments for patronage. Develop seminars that will be useful to solving social problems and ask agencies for sponsorship. They'll agree.

#9. Approach Training Consultants and Suppliers to Distribute and Follow Up their Proposals. Many companies do not have offices or representatives in the city where you live. Write to them to become their agent. They will send you as many proposals as possible to be submitted to government establishments and corporate offices. You can also help them to do the follow up at intervals and give them feedback. You can do the same thing for as many companies as possible. They will give you money to facilitate the distribution and follow up, and you can negotiate as much as 30% share of the profit from any business you help them to facilitate. Think about this.

#10. Help Companies Set Up Referral System. Most companies have no idea how to use referral strategy to acquire more customers. Please see my book titled: "Fastest Ways to Win Many Customers and Clients without Spending Much Money". It's devoted to helping businesses know how to leverage on referral strategies to make more sales.

Help companies to document and reward referrals. 'How did you hear about us?' The person he mentions, gets 10% of worth of purchase. Set the system to work for your client. You will boost their business when those who sent them buyers get paid from the purchases made. Work with car dealers, high cost items sellers, estate agents, etc. Place adverts with slogans, such as, "Do you want to buy expensive cars cheap?" Call me! Then give your contact details. When you get a call, you take them to your client car dealer. You get cut when they make sales.

#11. Public-Relations Agency. Help your clients to have easy access to journalists and media men. Politicians need to be in the limelight, organize interviews for them, Director Generals of head of government departments need publicity to let the world know what they are doing. Top business men need publicity for their products and services. Network by developing contacts with media practitioners on radio, television, print and social media to organize interviews, press releases, features and appearances for them. This will help your clients remain popular and in the public consciousness. You will be paid for facilitating such services.

#12. Consultancy Services. To be a consultant, you need to have an expertise in something, so you can market yourself as an advisor to persons who need help or assistance in that area. What experience for special skills do you have that others will be interested in when you share it with them? If you can organize this idea very well, then write proposals to individuals and companies, explaining what you can do to help them. They will invite you and you will do business with them. That is what consultancy is all about. What skills do you have right now that can be of value to someone is you serve them with it? Think! It could be as simple as teaching obese and overweight people how to eat right. Or show business owners how to do simple business accounting and book keeping. You can teach them how to operate their business on systems.

#13. Business Plan Consulting. The tool you need is your brain and your expertise. Business plan is crucial in obtaining bank loan and financing which many people requiring such cannot write. With your writing skills, spreadsheet know-how, and general business strategy, show clients how to present their best-laid plans and they will pay you. Ask bank managers, especially micro finance bank managers to refer traders and intending business people to you for assistance in packaging their business plans to meet their requirements and qualify them for loan considerations. They will send many clients to you.

#14. Business-Travel Management. Help book low-price tickets, keep expense records, manage frequent-flier miles and you will be paid. Traders, importers and busy companies will engage your services. Make sure you give them the cheapest rate and save them money better than what they can get anywhere else. They will retain your services. Companies, individuals and organizations are always looking for alternatives to save them cost.

#15. Help Business People to Develop Customer Database. It will surprise you that 90 percent of businesses have no means of capturing the information of customers that patronize them. They do not know the value of collecting the names, phone numbers, addresses, and email addresses of people who buy from them. You can become customer database manager to companies, big shops, small, medium and micro businesses. Help them take record of their buyers' contacts. You can do this by redesigning their cash receipt or invoice. You can tell them to fill the form where they will give that information, so you can inform them when next you have discount, clearance sales or price reductions.

To manage a database on behalf of the company, send customers' thank you messages, goodwill messages, seasonal greetings, and reminders of coming discounts. They can also use database to inform customers of any planned product or business promotion, introduction of new product line, etc. Become their relationship manager. Show them many ways they can use customer database information to make money and they will engage you.

#16. Help Estate Owners Who Have Houses that Nobody is Occupying to Attract Tenants. For example, if the estate is in a remote place, he can reduce the amount of rent to 60% it will attract people to take up the spaces. People will move in. Then after one year he can start increasing the rent. By the third year, he will be charging the normal rent and the entire estate will be filled up.

#17. Look for People Who Have the Market You Want to Reach. Do you have idea or services you want to sell to MTN or Glo or any of the telecommunication giants? Look for somebody who is already doing business with them, partner with him to sell the idea on your behalf. He will use his contact to bring out the business easily, and you will share the profit. It is better than you struggling on your own to get the company to buy your idea. Design good product and enter into partnership with someone who controls that very market you want to penetrate. It is better than you trying to make a fresh start. Bring two companies together to do business. For example, link tourist and travel agents. Link photographers and wedding planners, schools and book sellers, etc. you will profit from their transactions.

#18. Help Companies Send Thank You to Their Customers Daily. Do you know of any existing business that has the policy of sending thank you to all their buyers daily, or that has reward policy to their referrals? Key in there, fill that gap, do the business for them and you will have the job. Don't ask for salary but percentage from increased patronage.

#19. Sell Motivational, Inspirational and Christian Books on the Move. Collect classic motivational best sellers from book dealers (make good selection and buy cheap from wholesalers), then go to banks or big offices, markets, public transport (coaster or long buses) and sell directly to people. There are people who will love to read good books, but do not have time to go to bookshops to buy. Fill that gap and you will make money every day.

Stand where rich people frequent, and approach them as they come or as they leave the environment. Good spots are cable TV subscription centres- it is rich people that subscribe to DSTV, Kwese Sports, GOTV, etc. Stand at android phone service centres, busy market entrance and exit points, and busy plazas. Don't carry the material in your hand, put it in your bag and bring it out as you approach prospects. I guarantee you will make massive daily sales. You can recruit people to do this for you and pay them generous commissions.

#20. Connect Manufacturers and Distributors. Look for individuals and companies whose products are not selling, connect them to marketers and distributors and profit from the deal. Look for people with local product that are effective but not known. Show them how to repackage the product, and then link them to distributors and marketers. You will make money from the deal. Sometimes all what a product needs to start selling is to place them in stock with wholesalers and distributors to gain exposure with retailers to buy.

#21. Joint Venture/Strategic Alliance. Here you connect two companies together to do business and you get the lion share from the profit. You refer people to buy from a particular company and they pay you commission for every purchase the buyer makes with that company forever. To be able to make quality deals, you have to be creative, think in terms of innovation and find different ways to do things that many people are not thinking about. Find people who have market control, and people who have good product and services. Bring them together and profit from the transaction.

#22. Referral Business Services. Most businesses pay money to anyone that brings customers to buy their product. Negotiate to receive commission for as many times such a customer comes back in the future to buy. Never help anybody to sell any product or item without negotiating how much commission he will give you. Locate good dry fish distributors and link them with teachers in schools, company staff, civil servants, etc. they will buy in cartons. You will make money from every sales made. Target consumables and businesses that have repeat patronage.

Local companies pay to welcome customer and get their services introduced to them; (these new customers can even pay for a little friendly advice). Large- and small-scale manufacturers, supermarkets, electronic dealers, wood and building material dealers, machine tool sellers, etc. can engage you to introduce their new products to potential buyers as they walk around to choose the item they want to buy. You help the customer make good choice while the company makes sale and they will pay you well. Go and introduce this idea to them, they are not thinking about it now.

#23. Advert and Publicity Vendor. Paste posters, distribute handbills, place banners, make publicity and let people identify you with it. You will get calls regularly. Politicians, pastors, manufacturers, and protesters will patronize you.

#24. Seminar Promotion Services. Consumers are never tired of self-development information. Help people to promote and plan their informational seminars and workshops. You don't need to be an expert yourself; just schedule the speakers, reserve a location, promote the event, and get ready to collect the profits at the door.

#25. Design Programs cum Project and Approach Companies for Sponsorship. This is what concept developers do. Approach the media and advert agents of big companies in telecommunications, food and beverage sectors. MTN spends over 6 billion naira for adverts yearly and they are always looking for new ideas and concept to make money and popularize their products. Think of new things you can introduce to them. You never know what might happen. You must be a hungry fighter to succeed.

#26. Organize Your Own Seminars. You can organize seminars in your own chosen profession- food and confectioneries, dieting, sports, weight loss, marriages, women issues, etc. make the initial ones free. Organize seminars for NGOs. Get facilitators to collaborate with. Look out for needs and problem areas in the society and explore them. Sometimes you need not speak a word. Just organize and bring resource persons and facilitators. Charge moderate fees, they will deliver the lectures and participants will pay. Remember to record the training so you can sell the video. Package the training manual into a booklet and sell. Where possible make tape and CDs and sell, both hard and soft copy. Host the information in your social media handle, web or blog site and sell.

#27. Do Public Speaking. Many motivational speakers are springing up. Identify your area of competence and work hard to develop it. Look at the magnitude of income comedians are making today. Think of areas and things you are passionate about. If you're the type of person who can get the attention of a room easily, public speaking might be for you. Take advantage of every public speaking opportunity you can get, and be ready to speak for free. You can start by speaking to children in schools, churches and youth groups. As you gain experience you can start organizing seminars and workshops in the areas you have acquired competence.

#28. Tape Record Your Messages in CDs, DVDs, Videos, Podcasts. Marketing your articles and ideas give you publicity.

You can also document your speeches and publish them into a book, video and compact disks. If these ideas address family issues, diet, weight loss, health issues, marriage, relationships, fashion, unemployment, security challenges, children need, and business solutions, they will sell. Always think of what will solve problems for people in your community. Just experiment!

#29. Organize Talent Hunt Shows. Raw talents are abundant in Nigeria. Imagine what is now happening in home video, comedy, music and the show business in general. Organize one or better still, identify talents and introduce them to people who can sell them. You will always profit in-between. Telecom giants and breweries favor sponsorship of talent hunt shows.

#30. Explore Tourism Potentials. You can act as a tourist guide to foreigners who come into the country in large numbers. Print business cards and distribute to tourist firms, airlines and ticketing offices. You will be busy traveling and conducting tourists all over the country. Learn about interesting parks, historical centres, ranch, and games reserves; learn about places that tourists like to visit. There are many of them in Nigeria. Read tourist books and get more information from the internet.

#31. Daily Need Business. Engage in small everyday business like frying akara, pap, buns, donut, puff puff, and local delicacies. Think of the delicacy in the area where you live. Do it decently to suit the culture of that area. People will patronize you. A lot of people overlook the fact that there is big money in little businesses. If you can do this well, then approach companies that organize frequent events. You can handle cocktail and small get-togethers for families by providing the small chops.

#32. Be a Distributor. Not many manufacturers require you to make huge down payments or register with big sum of money.

You can either be a sub distributor with someone you know, or you go to a depot and start convincing major distributors to give you goods to sell. The town near you could be the depot for most goods made in the industrial cities. Go there and try. Most of these things depend on your boldness and power of negotiation. Try!

#33. Restaurant Delivery Service. Link with restaurant and fast food operators and help them to deliver lunch and snacks to busy professionals. Collect list of potential clients and call them up frequently to take their order. You can deliver the meal in half an hour and you will be paid from both ends.

#34. Market Your Skills Personally. If you are a teacher, security guard, marketer, etc. boast of your achievements and effectiveness to employers. They will consider and believe you will be useful and employ you. Write a letter to as many companies as possible; you will be surprised you will get calls.

#35. Become an Adviser in a Specific Area. Start by writing effectively on such topic and areas. Organize and host seminars and workshops in areas like security, marketing, pension or marriage. People will see you as an expert and helpful and they will begin to consult you. This happens especially if you can write books in such areas of interest. Just focus on helping others and never focus on immediate benefits that may come to you.

#36. Collect and Sell Items or Products that Make People Laugh. Laughter relieves stress. Tell potential buyers that laughter cures high blood pressure. Educate them that laughter improves health. People are looking for solution providers to their problem and challenges. Give them comic and humor books (get my book on "Humors that Make You Quake with Laughter"), funny short videos, and films. You can download many of these for free online. Compile and burn them into CD, or DVD, package decently and sell. They will buy instantly. Take it to offices, market stalls, shopping plazas, etc. Upscale by mass producing and link with marketers and distributors.

#37. Bed and Breakfast. Do you have a neat room you can rent out to travelers or tourist at a fee? This works particularly well if you live near an area that attracts regular travelers and tourists or where churches are having frequent conventions and meetings that attract large crowd and campers. Many of them will rent your room if it is cheaper than the nearby hotels.

#38. Supply Foodstuffs to Hospitality Industries. Supply chicken to the small hotels that can buy 20-30 pieces per week. If you have 50 customers, you can sell in thousands per week and make a huge amount of money. Don't compete with great producers, rather, target the small buyers. Again, collect on credit and make the supply.

Number Three: Internet and Online Businesses that Can Earn You Money

#1. Start an eBay Business. You need to get an eBay account with a PayPal to use for transactions. Collect old valuable items, decide how much you want to auction them and how long it will stay. The eBay website provides all the information you need to know to operate an eBay business.

#2. Go into Internet Marketing Full Time. The opportunities are enormous. Many business owners are not online yet and they are ignorant of the advantages it can give their business. Take it as your job to show them and you will charge them money. For example, link car dealers to advertise in websites that car buyers visit. Link hospitals that treat cancer or weight loss to websites that deal on such issues.

#3. Guide Companies that Have Website on How to Do Affiliate Partnership to Earn Commissions. You can also do the same thing on your own and earn commissions for finding the companies buyers online or offline. Google and research on this lead

#4. Social Media Marketing. Learn how to use the social media to market products and services since you are already on Facebook, Twitter; LinkedIn, YouTube, etc. Help companies to place their advert in websites that have high traffic. They will pay you because they do not know how to leverage on such advert publicity to expose their products to target potential customers.

#5. Start School of Social Media Marketing! Think of this as the same way people start computer schools, start school of social media marketing. So many companies are learning to advertise and sell their products online but do not know how to do it. They have beautiful websites but have no idea how to attract traffic and visitors to their webpages, each them. Teach them how to make their business and products popular in the social media. They will come or send their staff to learn and will pay you to do so. Read MULTIPLE STREAMS OF INTERNET INCOME by ROBERT ALLEN. The book alone will become your curriculum. You will have a wide niche market to serve. The world is moving towards the internet. Team up with experts to get it done.

#6. Go to Companies and Canvas for them to Build Website. Link them to someone who can build the website and share in the profit. Take the marketing very seriously and you will get customers. You can get the job and give to web designer at Fiver.com for $5. There are millions of businesses who still have not seen any reason to be online, and majority do not know how it can explode their business profitability. Educate them and secure their patronage.

#7. Link Entrepreneurs to Do Business Online. Link importers and foreign companies to advertise on websites of local businesses selling their kind of products.

#8. Help Companies Register Online Payment Account. Do this especially those payment options that enable complete transactions online internationally. Many people with good products to sell have no idea on how to get the automated payment systems that will enable customers pay electronically from anywhere in the world without leaving their seats. Many of those payment options are free and can be registered in minutes. Leverage on people's ignorance and they will pay you. Alternatively concentrate on getting jobs for someone with website design and host skills to handle the jobs and share profits made

#9. Information Downloads. Make money from information download from the Internet; package and sell as books but try to localize the information to make it culturally and contextually relevant. You can still make handouts, cards, pamphlets, almanacs, calendars, CDs, DVDs, Podcasts, Videos, etc. from the information gathered on the Internet. There are many self-development books that are begging to be shared with others. Get the permission of the authors and commercialize them and sell. Check YouTube for materials you can take advantage of legitimately. This is big money that few people are looking at.

#10. Blogging. If you enjoy writing, find a topic you're passionate about and start a blog on the topic. All you need is a computer, and some energy to consistently write. It can start as a hobby and turn into a business. Think and go in the areas of celebrity gossip news, relationships, dating, fashion, health and breaking news.

#11. Create an e-Book. If you have some special and extensive knowledge about a particular hobby, activity or skill, then put it to use and write about it. It maybe you know several different ways to cook particular meals. Or that you are very good at making special Christmas decorations. Or that you have extensive knowledge about taking care of a sick loved one, or maybe you know some special tricks in preparing meals for large or small families, just put this information down on paper.

It does not matter the number of pages. You can sell an e-book over and over again. It is easy as there is nothing to print or warehouse, it is read in PDF document in the computer. Buyers will pay online and download into their devices. Research on these for more information.

#12. Become an Internet Trainer. Believe it or not, there are still lots of folks including many senior citizens and retirees who don't have a clue on how to access the internet or where to go when they want to browse. If you're a tech whiz, you can teach these individuals how to navigate the information superhighway with ease as an internet trainer and they will pay you.

Give seminars, workshops, day-long courses or provide one-on-one assistance to top company executives who still are not internet literate in their homes. Tailor your training to their specific needs. They may only be interested in power point presentation, or skills to search information or send emails. Ask what they want to know and show them specifically. Simply send letters to as many company executives as possible; you will be surprised the number of responses you will get.

#13. Internet Advertising: If you have a blog, then you have got a great place to start selling advertising space. All you need to do is to focus on building up a strong community with quality contents and most of the time marketers will start emailing you with offers to place on your blog. Remember that you can always start a blog for free or little cost using WordPress. Meet people who have heavy traffic and large followers on their social media pages and help them get companies to advertise there. You will be paid constantly on commission as long as those ads remain there.

#14. Online Media Consultant. Do you like participating on message boards, Facebook, Twitter, and so on? Become an online media consultant and help people promote their products and services. Start small, help local businesses get a presence on Facebook and set them up on Twitter.

#15. Your Opinion Online is Money. Give your opinion and make money. Advertisers need to form consumer groups to help them determine if the marketing for their product will be right. Visit site like FocusGroups.com to see the ones that are appropriate with you. By filling out a survey, you can turn 10 minutes of your time into quality cash. Go to OpinionOutpost.com to get started.

#16. Web Content Development Services. Website developers always need strong writers to produce quality content for them. And they will sometimes pay top dollar for packages of several articles. Look for potential work on eLance.com. If you have any skill at programming or working with code, then a frustrated website owner somewhere will gladly pay you to take care of some problems he may be having. Try out the job postings on a site like upwork.com.

#17. Become an Affiliate Marketer. You can open a webpage in an established website and sell the product of other companies. You earn commission when people visit your website, click and buy the product. They have a system to track every purchase generated by your website. There are hundreds of Affiliate Companies online that you can join right now. Search here: www.ezinfocetre.com, www.clickbank.com, www.clixgalore.com, www.commission.com. Many of them have over 1000 merchants for you to choose from. Find affiliate that is visited mostly by women. (Women constitute over 80% of money spend on the internet).

#18. If You Want to Get Your Own Web Page, search here: www.godaddy.com, www.weeby.com, www.wix.com. Check out these websites they will help you in internet marketing. www.internetmarketingrules.com, they have free books you can download. www.hypnoticsellingsecret.com.

#19. Do online Freelance Writing Jobs. That's when you can pick up jobs doing freelancing for various functions. Try a site like FreelanceJobOpenings.com to see if there is a posting for something you will be able to do.

#20. Sell Jewelry Online. If you have a good eye for detail work, homemade jewelry can be quite profitable. There are many opportunities to sell such items through local gift shops or at sites like Etsy.

#21. Design Graphics Online for Clients. Lots of people need cool graphics for all sorts of reasons. Market your artistic talent to potential clients using a site like 99designs.com.

#22. Sell Photographs Online. The digital camera has got everyone into photography, and those photographs could be worth something to someone else. Upload them to a place like Flickr or iStockPhoto and see if anyone has a need to license them. All the same, you can sell your hot on the spot news images you are able to capture live with the camera on your phone?

#23. Sell Your Business Plan Online. Believe it or not, business plans are also among the things to sell to make money. It can be done on something as common as eBay. Like many other postings on the popular auction site, your ability to sell your idea on eBay mostly comes down to how well you put together your sales post. You can't imagine the number of people out there who desire to access the government loans for Small and Micro Enterprises but have no idea how to package their businesses to meet the guidelines to qualify. Go into business to help them and they will pay you.

Number Four: Events Planning and Promotion

#1. Become Sole Agent to Influential Society Weddings and Events. If the wedding will attract a lot of public interest, negotiate with the family and couple to give you the sole right to media coverage, an arrangement that will ban all journalists from videoing or taking pictures. Imagine the number of soft sell magazines and TV entertainment producers that will approach you.

Imagine what will happen if Ovation TV, or Bisi Olatilo Show will approach you for permission to cover the wedding of Dangote's daughter (or whoever is a top shot in your community)? He will come because you have negotiated and secured the right from the family. Think about the cash that will flow! Wayne Rooney made millions of Pounds by giving the sole coverage of his wedding to a magazine in UK. No one had done that before.

Think of the number of journalist, TV, radio, magazines, show hosts, local photographers that will want to take pictures of guests, and the fact that they will want to pay to gain access to the venue to do their business. Once it is a celebrity event people will be eager to see, then know there is money to be made. Be quick and be the one to make that money by engaging and reaching agreement with the organizer.

#2. Events and Party Planning. Target people that are planning naming, wedding, end of year events, house warming, birthday, burial, convention, children party and other ceremonies. Your customers are plenty. Many people who are throwing parties will desperately need your service. Let them know you can handle everything from invitations to the catering, from the entertainment to cleaning up afterwards, from the wine shopping to decoration. Take the stress off them and take their money afterwards. Advertise in soft sell magazines the moment you start making money.

#3. Children's Party Planning. Children do not want to miss their birthdays, and parents do not have the time to plan it effectively. Do parents a favor and plan their next children's birthday party. From hiring of Disk Jockey, to coordinating games, decorations and food, you're sure to be the life of the party by allowing parents to relax and have fun.

#4. Promote Events. Help people to market their program and promote their events like workshops, seminars, launchings, political rallies and campaigns. Publicize and people will consult you and pay for your work.

#5. Equipment Leasing and Rental Services. You don't need to own one yourself; play the go-between. Lease from the owner and rent to the user. Charge them and take your profit. Equipment here includes hiring of generators, food warmer, carpets for VIPs, musicals and sound systems, video, photocopy equipment, canopy and chairs, decorations, water pumping machines, coolers, pots, utensils, etc.

#6. Funeral Homes. Decoration of venue for lying-in-state. You can be well paid if you have good aesthetic sense. Do it so well such that people will desire to die just to experience your services. Rent materials on credit when you have a job and pay as soon as you are paid. A business of rebuilding tombs is a deal right now.

She simply visited her dad's grave side in a cemetery to drop some flowers and observe how old, shabby and unkempt some graves are. Instantly she conceived the idea that people will like it if they have the burial place of their loved ones built in marble and well preserved in beauty. With this, a new business is born, and patronage boomed. Why don't you look in that direction as you will have no competition yet?

#7. Decoration of Event Venues. You must have knowledge of how to use balloons and colors effectively. It is big money. Once you are known you will not lack jobs to do. Let them know you in your church, event centres, clubs, and offices. It usually holds on weekends and there are many society weddings and occasions that call for celebrations, and festivities going on everywhere. You can take advantage of them and make money. If you can't do it, then, get the job and give to others and get your commission. It is estimated that people in Lagos State spend as much as N4 billion every weekend on parties. You can get a piece of that cake, even in your small city.

#8. Photography. You don't need to own a shop to become a photographer. Rent a quality camera and start. Go to venues and churches and cover events like weddings, seminars, funerals and diverse celebrations. Take shots, print them out in a matter of minutes. There are so many instant digital photo printers today, buy one once you have the money. Attach yourself to marriage registries, liaise with them and become their official photographer, even if you come occasionally you will still make lots of money. Put your ear on the ground for seminars, conferences, church events, and all manners of social gatherings. People like wait-and-get photos.

Number Five: Office and Personal Services

#1. Mailing Services. Visit as many companies as possible and let them know you are available to help them speed deliver their mails. Remember, many of them have no messengers. Charge them lower than what courier companies charge, and they will always call you to pick up mail deliveries. Just have a good knowledge of the town or city. They are always looking for easy ways to send out proposals, post or pick letters from post offices, send out invitations, and all of that. Key in. Insurance companies, banks, pension managers and administrators, micro finance banks process and post bulk letters frequently and they need helping hands sometimes. Make yourself available. Advertise and you will get calls once they need extra hands.

#2. Office-Support Service. Typing, filing, sorting mail, entering data, and answering phones are just a few tasks an office-support service can perform to help out business owners with limited staff strength. Just let them know they can call you anytime they need your help. Go to business complex and hand out business cards to every businessperson in sight and get ready to work anytime the phone rings to call you up.

#3. Errand Runner. Go to a business complex and announce to every company represented there that you are available for their errands. From posting their letter, buying of recharge cards, depositing money in banks, delivering packages within town and buying of lunch to typing of letters at business centres. Don't you think you will have more than enough tips at the end of every work day for such services? Try it.

#4. Office Equipment and Stationery Supply. Supply-furniture, stationery and machines. Take catalogue from dealers, go round offices and show them. If you get sales, go back to that company and they will supply, and pay you commission. Go round offices and let them know you can supply them office consumables. Save them the cost of going to town to buy, you will be bringing for them. Leave your contact. You can always collect from sellers, deliver, collect the money, pay them back and keep the difference. Every office need stationery, ink for their photocopier and printers, pen, toilet papers, tea and coffee. Build your business around these areas.

#5. Medical Equipment Supplies and Installations. Solicit and get the contract, then meet the dealers to make the supply, collect the money, pay them and pocket the rest. You don't need to be an expert to do this. Just know how to study the catalogue or get someone explain for you how the machines work. Know that a company can always take over a prospect once you have made the initial contact that elicits buyer interest. You make money when he closes the deal. Employ yourself using these methods.

#6. Partner to Sell Second Handed Office Equipment. You can visit offices and homes and collect disused office equipment like desk-top computers, printers, furniture, refrigerators, and televisions. Buy them cheap, refurbish them and sell at higher prices. There is hardly any office without one condemned item or the other. Go to business centres and see for yourself.

#7. Executive Search and Specialized Staffing. Help busy clients find the right candidate for the job. Your job involves placing ads and conducting interviews to screen potential employees for clients. Put up the adverts, put on your best interviewing suit, and get down to business. You will get calls.

#8. Monitoring and Evaluation Services to Funding and Donor Agencies. Write to foreign donor, funding agencies, grant givers, Foundation and Philanthropists that sponsor projects in towns and villages and give money to local NGOs to appoint you to monitor and investigate how NGOs and people receiving their funds are using it. They will agree and engage you. They will pay. Just research, find them and write to them. Build on the suspicion that most NGO operators divert project funds for their private use.

#9. Help Companies Train their Staff. If you want to get results fast then help small business owners to train people who market their products including their shop attendants, receptionists, sales girls and front desk officers. Have you observed that most of these categories of staff have little understanding of simple office etiquettes, manners and customer relation attitudes? Also, train your own staff (if you have reason to employ any). Empower them to be creative and have reasonable autonomy. They will use their unique talents to move your business forward. Teach them to be good agents and representatives of your company.

#10. Become Foreign Investors' Adviser and Guide. Make it easier for foreigners to do business in your country. Gather information on individuals and companies that intend to invest in Nigeria, and request to give them information or statistics about the business and socio-economic climate in Nigeria. They will pay you for such report. A lady attracted European industrialist looking for where to invest to buy carbon certificate worth N6billion. Carbon trading is a whole new industry that many people are not looking into. Explore the untapped opportunities in Climate Change option.

#11. Bulk SMS Sender. Source to manage bulk SMS correspondences for companies, churches, and emergency messages for agencies dealing with the large membership or groups, etc. There are companies that want to reach out to their customers, meet and serve them. They will always call you to send their bulk SMS.

#12. Find Out What Companies Are Not Doing that You Can Start Doing for Them. Ask to be the one sending thank you text messages, writing letters to all the buyers for the day, help post letters, inform their clients of new welfare policy, etc. these are existing jobs that nobody is seeing.

#13. Selling Educational Materials. Get hold of recommended books for schools, especially primary schools and approach schools to supply them. You can collect from distributors and supply the books (focus on texts on compulsory subjects). You will be paid as they sell to their pupils and students and you will make lots of money. Most of the schools charge three times what is sold at street bookshops. Selling educational materials is a big business today.

Pencils, exercise books, recommended textbooks, graphical tables, and drawing equipment are some of the materials students cannot do without on daily basis. Negotiate with the school head teachers or the principals. You can be the sole supplier. A better way to make a kill is to custom design the materials with the school name and logo. Take the sample to them and they will place order immediately. You are bound to make a lot of money. Always target high fee-paying private schools.

#14. Help Private Schools Prepare their Exam Papers. During exams they will want to type and duplicate the examination papers for their students but do not have the time to go to business centres for it. Visit as many schools as possible and collect such jobs. Charge them well and you will make money. Help people and business get what they want; they will help you get what you want.

#15. Help Newly Established Private Schools with Ideas to Get More Pupils and Students to Register in the School. For example, convince the proprietor to give scholarship to two hundred students for one year in his school. That means they will study for one year without paying school fees (but will pay every other fee or levy). Let him conduct the test among schools where rich people attend. Give them admission with tuition free for two terms or the whole first year if you can. By the second year, they will start paying fees and you have two hundred students that you would not have attracted without such enticement. He will pay for your ideas.

#16. Go to Schools and Teach Teachers and Students How to Use Smart Board or the Computer. Computers have become part of everyone's life, not only in schools, or at workplaces, but in the home as well. Teach others how to using a computer; how to use it to prepare their lessons more efficiently and get more out of it. Many of them who can use it do not know how to use specific software programs. Take the proposals to the school and you will be called upon.

#17. Computer Training for Kids. Teaching children early, the basics of computer knowledge is one thing that parents are proud of. It helps to put kids at the head of their class, so approach the rich and well-to-do parents for that service and they will engage you.

#18. You Can Serve More than One Company at the Same Time. That gives you freedom to more, explore more and make more money. Get as many clients as possible and delegate surplus customers to others. Photocopy their receipts daily and work on it. Become business relationship consultant. Never agree to become a full-time employee to a company when you can render the same service to as many companies as possible and make more money.

Number Six: Editorial Services

#1. Proofreading and Editing Can Get You Money. Do you have strong and exceptional skills in grammar? Are you a creative writer with knack for spotting typographical errors and grammatical mistakes? Advertise with book publishers, magazines and newspapers. A good way to get a job is to take any newspaper, edit it thoroughly and take it to them to see the errors they are putting out to the public; they'll employ you

#2. Copyediting. Fact checking takes place here, and grammatical, stylistic and typographical errors are caught. Talk to magazine publishers for jobs.

#3. Proofreading. You work before the final piece is put out. The proofreader makes sure the copyediting changes have been properly made and no new errors are created in the process. Show book publishers errors spotted in their book.

#4. Developmental Editing. Are you skilled in developmental editing? Work with manuscripts, overhaul it to conform to standards in content and organization.

#5. Ghost Writing. Many rich people want to tell their stories. Many rich society women want to tell about their experiences. Partner to write and then share the proceeds after the book lunch. They have the money, you have the skills.

#6. Copywriting. Most companies put out bad ad copies that don't get attention. Their adverts or flyers are not noticed. Serve them and take their money if you have strong copywriting skills.

#7. Magazine Article Writing. Can you write compelling creative stories? Approach soft sell magazines. Sell your works to online article companies. Magazines and newspapers are good places to test your skills before publishing your book.

#8. Book and Material Editing. Advertise to edit works written by other people if you have good command of English. People are always looking for someone to proofread their written materials.

#9. Language Interpreters and Translation. You will get jobs with international organizations hosting seminars, foreign trade departments, embassies, etc. Get the news out about what you can do, and they will always contact you anytime they have an international event.

#10. Author Books. If you have the skills and talent to write books, self-publish and market them. If the work is good publishers will approach you thereafter.

#11. Be a Research Writer. Write articles for newspapers, magazines, journals, scripts for home video producers, radio and television stations. Search the Internet for companies that require such services. They will pay you in big money. This is a reality. Think up a fresh idea and sell them to a daily paper or magazine. They will give you a column on that. Create a unique style of writing and start. Don't mind the grammar, they will edit before publishing.

Number Seven: Simple Agro Related Ventures

#1. Utilize Empty Plots of Land Near You to Grow Fruits and Vegetables. Take permission from people who own empty plots of land that are not used for anything at the moment. You can plant pawpaw that can produce in three months. Get improved variety seeds. Even in the city, you see people planting banana tree along river water ways, and swamp areas. They make lots of money and they do not need permission from the council or from anyone to do that.

Maybe there is a large expanse of land in your family backyard (in the village), simply think of fast yielding fruits and vegetables you can use it to cultivate. Moringa has become a hot cake nowadays. There will always be people to come and buy off whatever you produce, no matter how far it is,

#2. Sell Animal Shit as Manure/Fertilizer. Go to all goat and cow markets, go to poultry farms, all pig farms, gather the animal droppings (shit) and bag them. Go and sell to farmers and vegetable farmers. It is richer and superior to inorganic fertilizer. Chemical fertilizers cause cancer, so organic manure is better.

#3. Plant Papaya (Pawpaw). Will it surprise you that at about October a Pick-Up Truck load of pawpaw sold for N160,000 to wholesalers in Abuja? Do you have a land in your village wasting? Use it to plant improved variety, hire truck and bring the product to fruit markets in the city, you will make money many times over or bring the wholesalers to come and clear it from your farm.

#4. Animal Inseminate (artificial breeding). Go and learn the process of making cow, goat and other animals to become pregnant without waiting for their normal cause of nature.

Everybody in animal husbandry would want your services since you help them multiply their herds faster. You will be in big business.

#5. Become a Distributor of Organic Manure from Farms. Go to poultry farms, pig farms, cattle kraals and tell them to bring their animal shit for you to buy. That is if you can't go round to gather them. They will be happy to make money from what could have been thrown away. Collect dung and excrements (shit), and bag them neatly as fertilizer. Farmers who require organic manure and fertilizer will be coming to you, or you will be supplying to them. You will make money out of it. Make it your business and keep supplying farmers and horticulturists. Meet people who cultivate fruits and vegetables at the gardens in their backyard and be supplying them manure.

#6. Culture Maggots. Maggot is the best food for fish. Fish farmers buy them as feed for their fish. It is easy if you will like to do it. Gather chicken droppings (shit), make it very damp in water, then make a shallow grave, line it with waterproof and pour the damp chicken shit on it, break few eggs on top of it to attract flies. Then cover it slightly.

The flies will excrete maggot and the maggot will increase in size after a few days. You will then scoop and wash them in a basket. Sun-dry and bag for sale to people who own fish farm. The more the chicken dropping you cultivate, the more maggots you harvest. You can do that continuously. It is a dirty job but like it is said, "Shit money does not smell".

#7. Pet Grooming Many people loathe bathing their pets and trimming their hair. Pet groomers perform these tasks for a fee. If you love dogs, and cats this can be good for you. Puppies are expensive, you know that.

#8. Pet sitting When people go on trips, they're often concerned as to what will happen with their pets. So, offer yourself as a safe place to leave their pets or be willing to go to their home to take care of their pets. This may even go hand in hand with your pet grooming business. Inform your neighbors what you can do if they need your service.

#9. Pet Walking. Many busy people leave their pets home all day but realize that those pets really could use a vigorous walk (and an opportunity to relieve themselves) during the day. Pet walking is a great opportunity for exercise, fresh air, and some pocket money if you have free time.

#10. Pet Yard Waste Cleanup For many people in suburban areas, cleaning up pet excrements is a real disgusting job. Instead of cleaning it up themselves, they might hire someone to do it regularly, two to three times a week. Check out people with pets. They may not have the time to rid their dog of steaks, or take them to the vet, you can do that for them and get their money.

#11. Supply Pet-Food Via Home Delivery. Once you've searched out pet owners in your neighborhood, start talking to them to be delivering pet supplies directly to their doors. Link up with vet stores to collect the supply and make the delivery.

#12. Food Preservation and Processing. Items like tomatoes, cocoa yam, maize, yam tuber, okra, pepper, banana, plantain are wasted in quantity during harvest seasons due to lack of adequate preservation methods. At such times their prices become ridiculously low. But you can cash into the opportunity by buying and drying them up. You don't have the money, but you can negotiate and partner with someone with money to do the business with you.

The nation needs effective storage facilities for agro products. A basket of tomato that sells for N500 during harvest season can sell as much as N23,000 at off season. Can you imagine what will happen if you have storage facility that can preserve hundreds of baskets just for a few months? Get investors to tap that goldmine.

#13. Invest in Renewable Energy Products. Read about renewable energy on the Internet. You will find lots of business opportunities there. You probably know about solar energy, bio-digesters, magic stoves, etc. the climate change and global warming challenges have brought innovations in products you can cash into.

Research and be representatives of those companies whose products are not selling in your environment yet. Act fast. Many government agencies can patronize you if you convince them that introducing the equipment for use will help improve the environment. It is all about taking initiative, and you never know. Convince a fish farmer who spends lots of money buying fuel to pump water to switch to solar powered electricity to pump his water. Then get a company that can install the solar panel and battery to render the services and get your cut of the profit. Many people do not even know solar powered water pump exist. You will save the person huge cost and he will be grateful to introduce you to other customers.

Number Eight: Jewelry and Artwork Business

#1. Jewelry Making. Ankara jewelry making is getting popular. There are many ways of getting into the jewelry business and many different types of materials with which you can do your work. Working in metal will probably require the most in the way of specific tools. You need to be able to heat the metal to manipulate it and you need metal working tools to cut and engrave it. But there are many other materials that you can work with to make jewelry—glass, plastic, beads, feathers, even wood, to name just a few. You can always find where to learn, or help the producers sell their products. Either way, you will make money.

#2. Sell Local Beads and Bangles. Collect as common in different cultures and tribes. Some people who are traditionally inclined will buy. Sell accessories that go with traditional clothes. These include handmade beads that women now love to wear. Learn to make them yourself. Select beautiful and attractive colors. Meet people who can teach you. You can use your free time to do it

#3. Become and Agent to Local Jewelries Makers. Go to Igun Street, in Benin City, Nigeria and negotiate with the local bronze makers to become their agent. Collect their work at cheap price, and take it to other cities to sell, negotiate with shop owners at airports, major supermarkets and art shops. Tourists love to buy them at high prices. Do the same with artists, painters and sculpture and local Jewry makers. All you need is to establish credibility and trust. Also meet people who will like their necklace and bangles customized with their names. Then get expert goldsmiths to mold with such inscription and you can make good money out of it.

#4. Collect Art Work from Artists- Get their paintings, sculptures, and carvings and resell them elsewhere. Many of them keep their works for months without being able to sell them. You can negotiate and buy cheap from them and display at supermarkets, tourist resorts, furniture show rooms, and shopping malls where rich people patronize, and you will sell them at higher cost.

Number Nine: Exercise and Fitness Business

#1. Exercise Teacher. Do you have the skill to teach an exercise class? Go to gyms, health and fitness centres springing up everywhere in rich neighborhoods and you will find work. Talk to every overweight person you meet on the street. They will invite you to their homes. Then minutes of massage is better than an hour of jogging. Tell them this.

You can also find people who do not want to go to the gym that you can train from home as a personal trainer. Give massage to people for a fee. Women love it. Their husbands do not want to do it for them, the shops where they can get the treatment charge exorbitant fees, come in-between and talk to them and do it in the comfort of their homes. They will pay you handsomely.

#2. Self-Defense Instructor. You can never feel too safe or secure. People of all ages and backgrounds can benefit from the self-defense skills you can teach them. Taiichi, Karate, or simply basic safety-awareness skills will be appreciated in these days of insecurity. Just approach people with a letter, proposing the benefits of your services. They will engage you.

#3. Personal Trainer. Target overweight and obese people, including children. They know they need exercise to keep fit but do not have the discipline to start any. Help them. Advertise your services in places where everyone goes, like restaurants and grocery stores. Having a website is a good idea. Remember that people want some privacy in their decision-making when it comes to keeping fit. They can go to your website and determine if your approach to personal training would work for them.

#4. Mobile Massage. A good massage is far preferable to jogging or running or other strenuous exercises. Advertise your stress-relieving services at local workout clubs, gyms, spas and physical therapists' offices. Be ready to serve people in their homes and you will get a lot of jobs. Satisfied clients will tell their neighbors and friends. Target rich folks so you can charge higher fee. Learn it.

#5. Health Counseling. Run a centre to counsel people about nutrition, run minor community health and dispensary that will be useful to community women, (nursing mothers, and pregnant women) and ageing populace. People are afraid of diabetes, cancer of all types, eating disorders, high blood pressure, hypertension and such related lifestyle diseases. Cash in and fill the gap.

All you need is the right knowledge and information, help people who are dying out of ignorance. Teach diet and nutrition. Many folks are hooked on rich-killing foods and they think they are enjoying life not knowing it is a matter of time before the cancer starts showing up on their body; educate them.

#6. Attend to Retirees Need. Meet retirees' need so they don't retire into idleness. Design programs to help them invest and manage their gratuity profitably. Many of them need entrepreneurial skill, how to invest or what to invest in so they don't lose their money through wrong investments decisions.

Number Ten: Personalized Services

#1. Run School of Leadership, Entrepreneurs and Innovations. In fact, whatever services you are rendering, always add training to it. Train people to be able to do what you have the skills to you. That is the fastest way to start consultancy services without money. Teach people how to add uniqueness to what they do to start attracting more customers. Many people are unemployed because they do not know how to take action and initiatives. Many retirees are afraid because they do not have skills or idea on what to do next after they are retired. They will call you to train them.

#2. Private Investigation. Help big men and busy wives watch their daughters or children's movement. Help off station husbands monitor their wayward wives, you will be paid. As a private investigator, make your mark in the industry by keeping a keen "eye" on other people's activities. Clients include attorneys gathering evidence for a case, or individuals seeking information about a significant matter will engage you.

#3. Help to Facilitate Loan. Help people to access loans from government lending agencies, cooperative societies, thrifts and clubs that can disburse funds. They will pay you both for information and assistance rendered.

#4. Debt-Collection Service. Identify all money lenders, especially those in usury business and ask to be their debt collector. They will allow you to follow up with their stubborn debt defaulters. You get paid when your clients get paid by the people who you influenced to pay them. As a debt collector, you help give some persistence in tracking down clients' delinquent debtors. They do not have the time to go looking for them. Without your services their money will be lost.

#5. Start Extramural Lessons and Professional Exam Coaching Classes. You can target people sitting for NECO, WAEC, GCE, JAMB, ICAN, TOEFL and other professional exams. There is about 85% failure in school certificate and university matriculation exams. People are desperate, and they'll come. Recruit teachers and they will do the job while you coordinate.

#6. Organize Private Home Lessons. Helping school children and students to enhance the mastering of their school subjects and pass tests and assignments can be lucrative. Teaching math, tutoring in English, Physics, Biology and Chemistry are simple and free to start. Get connected to your rich neighbors and their friends. Get referrals from anyone you know that work in well-paying establishments, they are the ones that can pay very high for you to coach their children. To get clients, go to the homes of rich people and ask them to allow you teach their children. Most students are poor in English and Mathematics. These are compulsory subjects and many people will welcome that idea. Go to the school environment and try this out.

Approach parents as they come to pick their children after school. Talk to potential clients in church after service. You can know rich people by the type of cars they drive. Don't be intimidated in taking your chances. You can print a notice and paste it in public places where it can be seen. With your phone numbers there, expect to get calls and you will. Holiday lesson is now the in thing. You get the job and employ the person to teach the subject. You don't need to be the teacher to be involved in the business.

#7. Tie and dye. It is easier to learn. Even within three weeks to one month you can learn it and start with very little income. Many people are into it and can teach you at very little cost. It sells if you can make good artistic designs.

#8. Driving Lessons. There are many people who want to learn driving. Rent an old car and teach them. They will pay for the lessons and the practice (test driving). It is a good way to earn income.

#9. Modeling. If you have what it takes in terms of beauty and physique, you can go into modeling. It is a good profession for people with intelligence, beauty and manners.

#10. Windshield Repair. To find potential clients for your windshield-repair business, canvas at local parking, used-car lots, plazas, shopping malls' parking spaces, etc. for cars with cracked, chipped windshields. A basic repair kit enables you to offer clients better alternative to new windshield.

#11. Used-Car Inspection. Hang around car dealers. Most buyers, especially ladies are novice at assessing and inspecting new or used cars.

Sometimes, it takes a little more than a kick at the tires to evaluate a used car. With some basic mechanical know-how, used-car inspectors can help steer clients away from costly buying regrets. Satisfied customers will always refer others to you.

#12. Mobile Mechanic. People have car breakdowns on the road. Make it a business to help them. Give your contact to as many car owners as possible. They will keep it safe, because it won't be long before they need your services. Just be ready.

#13. Seamstress/Tailoring Services. Show clients fashion design collections to choose from, then take the job to a tailor and get your cut. Rich people will patronize you.

#14. Hairstyling. This is a popular business, especially among ladies and it is quite lucrative. If you have skills in this area, focus on giving home services to rich clients. They will pay you and give you referrals easily.

Number Eleven: Modern Ways to Make Money Easily

In today's economy, the trend of working has changed. Since the advent of internet and advancement in technologies, many people have created jobs for themselves working from home. They no longer need to report to the office by 8am and return by 5pm running the rat race.

People now have jobs across continents and can serve their customers and clients from anywhere in the world and still make their money. Work at home jobs, freelancing and other money-making jobs requiring certain (often minor) skills and capabilities that can earn you reasonable income.

The beauty of these is that your clients can be sourced from any part of the world if you know how to put yourself out there on the internet. Once you are online, you are opened to global market place and they are in billions, but you must know how to attract the right people who need what you offer to look in your direction

#1. Write and publish a Kindle eBook. You can research and write an eBook on any desirable topic and sell it online on Amazon Kindle store and make money. As you may know, the Kindle app is now available on almost any device (laptops, iPads, smartphones and Kindles. With this platform, you are opened to the global marketplace.

You can price your eBook from one dollar to as much as 20 dollars and you can earn as much as 70% commission from every book sold. The most important factor that makes anyone successful with eBook is to write on subject matters that has value to readers. You focus on issues that solves problems for readers, that teaches them new skills, that educates them on something they are ignorant of and want to know. How-to-books, secret of books, etc. and presenting them in acceptable eBook format- basically PDF.

Get someone to design an attractive cover. You do this cheapest in Fourer.com or Fiver.com where anything can be done for you at $4 or $5 dollars. Then try and get reviews so it comes up high in search engine results. Once the work is done, you will earn residual income on it for years to come. Google this and see what it comes up to. You can do it: "How to write a nonfiction eBook in 21 days".

#2. Affiliate Marketing. You don't need to have your own product or services to own an affiliate, you simply promote other people's product and services and attract visitors and direct them to that website to buy. There is no limitation, you can promote popular brands products from Walmart, iTunes, Starbucks, and including products from smaller companies. When they do, you receive commission, sometimes up to 50%.

You look for products that pay higher commission and have higher price and promote the product in your website, your blog, your social media handle like Facebook, LinkedIn, and in any other article you write and publish.

Check out these link who pay regularly and faithfully: RakutenLinkshare ; Amazon (here you can promote books, car parts, audio books, video games, clothing, kitchen tools, just anything sold on amazon) Clickbank (there are thousands of products to choose from and you can get commissions as high as 75%); JVZoo(there are different types of products you can promote, ranging from cooking, business, education, travels, gambling to foreign language, just to mention a few).

#3. Help People Learn a Language. If you live in the city try and organize a French language class, advertise you want to teach Chinese language (you don't need to speak the language, get someone who can speak and partner with him to teach the audience you will attract). I tell you the business relation between Nigeria and China is growing fast, and many traders and importers who troop to that country will like to understand a few Chinese vocabularies that will enable them to communicate and do business better when they travel. You will be surprise the market exists waiting for someone to take the initiative.

Ambassadors, diplomats, foreign workers who do not speak English are here in large numbers with their families. They all want their children and wives to learn how to speak English language. Write them a letter to tutor their children in English and see the kind of response you will get instantly. You can make it faster by paying them personal visit, ask for audience with them and state your case. The need is there, and they will give you the job. You will earn big money instantly for a few hours job.

Look at all the opportunities that exist among construction workers and international employees from non-English speaking countries. They want basic communication to be able to go to the market and move freely on the streets. You can approach the embassies to help them understand the dynamics of our local politics.

#4. Tutor or Give Lessons in Variety of Things. Are you fluent in another language, a math genius, talented chef, a gifted pianist, guitarist, or a professional in music and dance? Whatever you're good at, there is in need of your service. Your job is to find them and help them! Teach people to tie head scarf, 'gele' for big parties and occasions.

Provide the service and make good money from it. You can write an eBook on any unique skills you have and sell it online if you know how and it's easy. Popular areas still remain cook book, health and weight management book, diet book and all of that. The point is, find out what people will like to know, including things they will like to know but do not know that they need to know it, then, teach them and collect their money.

#5. Financial Intelligence Coach, Manager and Trainer. Teach people financial literacy. Read The Rules of Wealth by Richard Templar, and Robert Kiyosaki's Increasing Your Financial IQ and start teaching individuals and organizations how to practice the principles of good financial management. How many organizations or individual salary earners do you know that pay themselves first no matter how much they owe in debt? Become a consultant by showing people how to discipline their habit and know how to save and invest wisely.

Send out letters and you will be sure to get calls. Try it now. Financial management adviser is a development that people are making a living from now. You don't need an office. Make people realize the importance of financial illiteracy and the fact they will remain poor if they fail to change. They will listen; just give yourself a corporate packaging. Nobody asks for your certificate before listening to you when you are talking sense.

You will have lots of clients from intending retirees, civil servants, schools, company, charity organizations, traders, general businesses. Many people have poor spending habits and do not know how to control it, many have no understanding on saving and investment matters. People are making money mistakes; they have worked for twenty years and have no savings. Despite having good income, they are constantly broke. Many workers are very close to retirement age and have achieved nothing. The point is that only few people understand finances and the rule of wealth and if you organize a seminar on the topic, many people will show up.

#6. Freelance Travel Agent and Tourist Guide. The internet has brought lots of changes to the traditional travel agent business. No matter how complicated a trip may be, it can be arranged successfully at the click of the button. Just have collaborations with other professionals, driving web traffic to them, as well as send them clients and make your cut of the profit.

As a freelance travel agent in these days of internet, all you need to know is to provide information to potential or prospective visitors, travelers or tourists. Your job is to promote tourist destinations in your nation or place by writing about them in your blogpost, and then when tourist or travelers contact you, you give them information and when they come you make adequate arrangement to make their stay comfortable.

Arrange hotels, get good taxi cabs, or bus to convey them, and have knowledge of places of interest they can visit. Help them out when there is issue with flight arrangement, tickets and any security concern they may have. If you do your job well, you will make money. Tourism is now the economy of the 21st century.

#7. Document Translator. If you studied languages, if you can speak different languages then you have a job waiting. Translators translate text from one language to another. Perhaps you studied French, Spanish, Germany, Portuguese, or even your local language. There are always people looking to find someone help them translate documents. Embassies, and international organizations, government ministries, agencies and departments do have jobs too. It's a straight forward job and if you have the talent and skills for it, you can make a huge money.

#8. Infographic Designer. Infographics have become a more powerful tool to visualize detailed information. Nowadays, people do not have the time to go through web articles thoroughly, so the Infor graphs talk to them quickly. If you have creative talent in designing visually appealing infographics, then you have lots of opportunity to make money. This simply means information graphic (representing text in pictures and making the message clearer).

Infographics are visual designs that help to explain complicated data in a simple way to grab the reader's attention. For example, tweets with images receive more clicks and retweets. It has been proven that marketing materials with visual content is more effective than text-based marketing. Also, publishers that use infographics grow traffic 12% faster and gets more attention from readers.

#9. Voice Actor (Voiceover Jobs). Voice actors provide voiceovers, and there are many opportunities for you to make money. There are people who have written books and will like to turn them into audiobooks. There are radio stations and advert agencies looking for someone with a nice voice to help them with jingles. Look for those who do animation works, games that want to give voice to their work.

There are individuals and companies with websites that want to develop video to explain their products and services to their audience; they are your target market. These are jobs you can access if you act boldly and talk to companies, artists, business people, authors, and they are everywhere. Your voice doesn't have to be special.

Simply let people know what you can do and how what you can do will help them promote their business. You will charge them and make big money. Turning a book to audio tape is nothing more than reading the book chapter by chapter till the end. That's all.

#10. Set Up an Online Store. You can make money from your own online store from the comfort of your home, it is very easy to set up! Many people make decent full time or part-time income with online storefronts. Here are a few favorites sites: Amazon, eBay, Zazzle, Cafe Press

#11. Make Money with Your Blog. Setting up a blog is easy with Wordpress.com. You can blog about anything- food, parenting, dating, relationships, fashion, business, travels, cosmetics, marketing, and celebrity gossips, just anything. That's where many people make their money. It does not take any time. The good thing is that if you can't write, look for someone who can write. Your blog will attract visitors, and you must have a product to sell to them, and the skill to convince them to buy or direct them to another site (where they will buy other people's product or service), that is if you promote another person's product.

#12. Graphic Designer. The demand for graphic designers is increasing daily because not many people has the skill. They are constantly wanted by companies, business centers, advert agencies, newspaper houses, retailers, and website owners. You can learn this skill from the roadside and it does not require any official training.

#13. Statistical Analyst. Can you interpret quantitative data, or design statistical models for research problems? This also involves knowing how to maintain databases and ensuring the validity of such data. Did you study mathematics, accounting, and statistics? These are areas you can develop your skills and start talking to managers in companies, non-profit organizations, and international development organizations. Statistical analysis is wide, and you may need to specialize either in marketing, health, engineering, or economics data.

Many companies are looking for someone with the ability to accurately analyze their data, many organizations have no idea how to keep accurate data and if you can help them organize and manage their data and statistics, you will have jobs to do. Look in the direction of research firms, consultants and marketing firms. Talk to companies writing proposals and making bids for tenders that want to package a comprehensive proposal for big projects.

#14. Software Engineer. You don't need to have a high degree to understand this. The way you learn website design is the way you can also master software engineering if you have enough interest. The good thing is that it pays and the demand for software engineers has ever been increasing because it is a special skill.

Now, every businessman likes to own a website and app, as well as have a formidable presence online. They need appropriate software for their business. The funny thing is their ignorance about available helpful software they can use to leverage their business operation and systems. So, you already have lots of customers waiting for you.

#15. Waste to Wealth Initiatives? All the plastic bottles (bottled water, soft drink, juice bottles) you see lying around everywhere constituting environmental nuisance, disused sachet water flying and dirtying the environment, canned drink and food beverage containers, broken glass and bottles on the roadside as you travel the road (don't pray for coca cola and brewery distributor trailer to fall), scrap metals of all sorts, the waste from vegetable markets, etc. all constitute wealth if you know what to do with them.

Go to work collecting these items that are available in super abundance, find where to sell them. Ask the scavengers around waste bin and they will give you information. Employ people to gather these materials, pay them and go sell them. Little enquiries will show you the wealth around you that you are not paying attention to. Besides, you will find commendation and even partnership from environmental activists.

Chapter 2

Entrepreneurial and Self-Employment Skills to Outsell Competitors
It will help if you are familiar with the following fundamental facts:

#1. Before You Begin Anything Prepare Adequately, No Assumptions Please: Develop yourself and acquire relevant competence. Emphasis has shifted to skills and capabilities. The question you must be ready to answer is, "What can you do?" Certificate means nothing if you are not competitive or have nothing of value to offer.

Happily, you don't always need to go to school to learn, the internet is there for you to get any information on anything under the sun easily. The problem is that most people are afraid to take the pain to prepare or develop themselves before venturing into anything. If you can't read to develop yourself, you will live poor and disadvantaged.

#2. Self-Employment Gives You Freedom: It affords you the opportunity to do what you

want to do, when you want and for whom you want. You are in control of your financial destiny. Nobody can fire or downsize you when you are self-employed. However, this freedom comes at a big price. If you are to succeed or fail, it's all up to you. Take up the option to determine what happens to you and your finances.

#3. There Are Many Businesses You Can Start Without Money: All you need to succeed is the ability to take profitable business and entrepreneurial initiatives. Learn how to engage your minds and creativity to birth new ideas. Many graduates just do not know how to think, the ones that can think are scared to death, and they don't want to think.

Read books that can open you up to new realities. Learn negotiation and deal making skills, learn to take action on ideas that come to you or information you stumble into in your reading and research. Learn to sell items, ideas, services that other people can provide. All these abilities will help put money in your pocket.

#4. Take Vocational Skills Seriously: Take advantage of any opportunity to learn new skills be it soap making, poultry or carpentry. Most experiences are useful at the moments you least expect they should. Nigeria is emphasizing on agro business and any agro skills you can lay your hands on will be helpful. Take your time and learn fish farming, fish feed, poultry feed production, trading on agro products, etc., they will become useful one day.

#5. Develop the Ability to Take Initiatives: Most talented people are poor and helpless because they lack courage to take up a venture that may give them a chance to succeed. Many people are fearful and timid and cannot just take that necessary step. So many cannot get over the mentality of comfort of salaried-office job, even when they have to remain idle for five years to find one. The business owners you desire to work for are not necessarily better or more intelligent than you. The difference is that they took risk with their life and paid the price to be where they are today. Your greatest assurance of security and greater future may be when you take that initiative. Forget your degree and ego, venture into that enterprise and in five years' time, you will thank God you did heed this advice.

#6. Be Proactive, Notice Things and You Will Know What to Do: Pay attention to your environment and you will always find a niche you can work on. Value curiosity and gather useful information you can package and sell to people. Render services that make people's life better, easier, faster, or more meaningful. Always think of how you can add value to people, products and situations.

#7. Identify Your Gift: Though you can learn and acquire new skill in any area you are interested in but you will always do better if you find out what you are born to do. In what skill, talent, or area of life are you specially gifted? If you can't find out what you are passionate about, you will never have specific direction, and people will use you to achieve their dreams.

Know early enough what you are born to do. Define your life and what you want from it. Streamline your desires, target what you want to do, and never be a generalist. Identify the type of customers you want to serve and people's needs you want to meet. If it is not clear in your life, you will not succeed. Your work and assignment are inside of you, you are likely to discover them in the areas you are naturally gifted. Engage your spirit to find out what you are born to do. Take the time and do it. Do soul searching and the Spirit of God might talk to you?

#8. Learn How to Be Purposeful with Your Life: Don't start a journey to nowhere. Seriously plan your life. Many people never sit down to plan their lives. Have set targets, have worthy goals you want to achieve, have strong objectives of useful things to fulfill in your life. Many people have no such ambition therefore, they don't have any drive or vigor towards anything.

Lack of clear written goals in life is the number one reason for failure. 95% of failures never write down their goals and 95% of people who have clearly written goals achieve them and are successful. Learn how to write down yours goals now, I mean today before you go to bed. If not, you are threading the path of failures.

#9. Do Things Differently: You will only succeed when you do things differently. Take what someone else has done, and tweak it is a unique way to get a different version of it. Never follow conventional wisdom, don't do things the same way every other person does.

Be creative and have special understanding on issue and apply it in a way that many people are not thinking about. Be unique, be original, enterprising, innovate, and creative in adding values even to ordinary everyday things and they will become especially different. If you serve food in restaurants, use vegetable and fruits to design the edge and surroundings of the dish to make the meal more appealing and attractive to the eye. Be artistically creative with food and vegetables and see how customers will rush your place.

#10. Cultivate Creativity: Experiment with new things and think out of the box to come up with new ideas. Think of values you can add to improve what already exists to make your product unique to attract patronage.

Engage your mind and unusual concepts will come up. President Robert Mugabe said, "If ladies can shave their eye brow and use pencil to draw a line on it, then why don't they shave off the hair on their head and use pencil to draw any hair design they like?" He might be derogatory, but believe me, tomorrow, any of the super model, or icon megastars will proudly experiment with such absurdity and before you know it, another industry is born. Look at the fashion craze all over town and tell me how they came about? Cultivate positive creativity and market it.

#11. Spend Time and Effort to Acquire Marketing Skills: Sales and marketing skills are essential to success in business and many other endeavors. Market yourself to potential employers; you pick products and market them to potential buyers and market your services to potential clients. Start reading, start attending seminars on sales and marketing, it will do you a world of good. Learn to network to get what you want.

#12. Think of New Insights: Always think of insights you can take advantage of to make progress. Look into people's businesses and observe what they are not doing that could have earned them money or save them some cost if they start doing it. Take the proposal to them and share in the gain they will make from implementing the idea you give to them.

#13. Consistently Look for Breakthrough Ideas and New Thought Pattern: Brainstorm with yourself or join a mastermind group to share and analyze ideas you conceive. There must be a different way to do what is being done. In what new ways can innovation be introduced in the way businesses serve their customers and can they pay you when you share your observations with them? Write down the ideas that rush into your mind. If you engage your mind for uncommon ideas, the Spirit inside you will bring new solutions that many people have not seen. Always look into the inside of your mind for unique ideas.

#14. You Make Money Faster by Selling Things that People Need than Attempting to Get a Job: A single vacancy can be targeted by hundreds or even thousands of applicants. With over 40 million unemployed graduates in the job market, your chance of getting a decent job is slim. Most people never realized this when they put themselves in the job market. Never let the thought of comfort from salaried job deprive you of what you might become by risking going into business for yourself.

#15. Have Strong Love for the Customers You Serve: Think of the benefits you can bring to your customers. Buyers will always go to the person who gives them the best value, who reduce price and serve them in a way that makes them happy. Focus on how to do them good. Your focus is NOT on you nor on your product, but on your customers. You will do well in business if you can conquer selfishness.

#16. Never Act As If You Know It All: Learn as much as you can from others on the best ideas or strategies to improve customer service and build up your business with what you have learnt. Copy from people doing better than you. There may be need for you to bring in people to help you bring your ideas to light.

Never let your dream die because of fear of someone outsmarting or edging you out. Success is not about you. You can team up with other bright minds to make your endeavor successful. Think of the tens, and possible hundreds of people whose welfare and livelihood might be positively impacted if that dream becomes successful. Go into entrepreneurship, not for your sake, but for the sake of others whose destiny is tied to it.

#17. Get Skills that Are Relevant to Today's Economy: Retrain yourself in marketable skills. Follow the trend in modern economy, watch how technology affects development and position yourself well so that you are not placed out of significance. Things change fast in this new millennium. Remain very current in event and global trends. Your approach should be constant and never-ending learning. Improve yourself regularly and be in tune with the scheme of things in your chosen profession and trade.

#18. Be Proactive with Your Life and Leave Nothing to Chance: Determine if you are going to create your own jobs or work for someone else. Learn effective job hunt strategies and have alternative plans to create jobs for yourself. You have job security if you work for yourself.

#19. Have Multiple Skills: It is always advisable that you consciously develop yourself into a multi-dimensional human being. Develop yourself to be able to do many things but be known for one major thing that you can do most expertly. Have skills that you will use to serve business people, companies, government and individuals and they will pay you money. It could be technical, vocational or intellectual skills. So long as you will be able to commercialize it effectively. Always think, "What can I do to make people pay me?" Money is paid to services rendered".

#20. Read Good Books and Keep Good Company: The books you read have a lot of influence on you. Carefully select quality self-development books. If you are not constantly learning and improving, you will not remain relevant or valuable for long. The speedy technology changes and fast pace of economic development makes constant learning imperative.

#21. Surround Yourself with People Who Can Inspire You: Camp around people who look hopeful and active with their lives. Keeping company with negative minded people will destroy your hope; damage your ambition and the zeal to move forward with life. Have mentors, guide, and people who will challenge and motivate you to greater heights. Don't neglect this factor.

#22. Mind Your Thinking Pattern: Your life unfolds according to the things you think about. Your present and future are built based upon the thoughts and imaginations of your mind. So, carefully take control of your thought and you may as well determine the direction of your life. If you don't understand the powers of your mind, especially your subconscious mind, you will wallow in failure, self-sabotage, mediocrity and limitations and will not know why. Learn how to get rid of your negative and limited thinking because you will never succeed with a wrong mindset.

#23. Have Staying Powers to Overcome Failures, Disappointments, and Setbacks from Mistakes: You must have persistence, perseverance, commitment, and dogged determination to succeed in life. If you quit easily you will never make it. Always rise up whenever there is a knockdown. There will always be but get going.

#24. Have Personal Sense of Responsibility: Take your destiny in your own hands and do nothing but the best you can do. Your success or failure is in your hands and not in the hands of the government. Love your country and pray for the leaders because you cannot prosper in a nation you hate. Be honest, upright and responsible. You cannot afford all the foolishness and stupidity exemplified by following in wasteful spending on fashion, music, relationship and all such negative indulgences. You will get it right only when you let God guide you. Leave in honest reverence for God and all will be well with your business. You can be a self-made millionaire.

#25. Plan Big, Start Small and Build Up: Life starts small and grows progressively, and so is business. Mansions and skyscrapers have deep foundations, and it picks up from there. Nobody starts building from the top. It is from the bottom up. Even giants are born as babies, not as six footers. The tendency to start business on a large scale when you have no experience to manage it is one of the reasons for large scale failure in new business startups.

#26. Be Determined Never to Join the Millions of Unemployed: To be able to help yourself, you must take the resolve never to join the battalions of people waiting for non-existent jobs. Resolve to help yourself and create your own job. It is very possible.

#27. Attend Seminars and Workshops: Seminars are good sources of information, training and capacity building, especially those ones that teach life and business skills. Most of them are free, and where payment is required, pay. It's a good way to invest on yourself. Ignorant kills your business.

#28. Save Money, However Small: A wise man said that if you can't save money then the seeds of greatness are not in you. Your allowance is little but putting some money aside every month will give you a head start. Take off the percentage you want to save as you receive any payment. Don't save the remnant after you have spent. Remember, anyone who wants to help you with money will always ask to know how much you have on your own. If you have nothing, he will believe you can't manage his resources too and so he will give you nothing.

#29. Associate with People Who Are Greater than You Are: Hook up with like minds that can inspire and challenge you towards greatness. People who can trigger the greatness in you to show up. Your association either makes or mars you.

#30. New Technology Source of Wealth: Online and internet transactions offer anybody anywhere the opportunity to make money with little or no skills. The internet has opened lots of legitimate money-making opportunities. Download articles, subscribe to newsletters, read blog posts, and other free web resources from Google and YouTube. The world of wealth is literally at your fingertips, if you can use your smart phone then you can do it.

#31. Be brave and Confident: Without courage, confidence and faith in one's ability, it is impossible to achieve or accomplish anything worthwhile in life. Those are the attitudes that help someone make a mark in life.

#32. Have the Attitude of Self-Reliance: Independent spirit helps get things done. The desire to live off other people's sweat is one of the reasons for under- achievement. However difficult, aspire to get things done without depending on other people. It doesn't mean you can't seek help when needed.

#33. Stay Away from Anyone that Belittles Your Dreams and Aspirations: Be sharp to recognize when you are in a wrong company. If you don't have this ability, you will fall under negative influence. People who look down, mock your dream and decisions are not your friends. Keep off them.

#34. Get Professional Qualifications: This will improve your chances of practicing certain professions. It also comes handy if you want to work for yourself or others. People still value professional qualifications as it often opens doors to opportunities.

Chapter 3:

Understanding Why Small Businesses Fail

You must first study why over 80% of every new small business fails within one year and 95% within five years. It could be risky starting new businesses, but you will succeed if you understand the difficulties than when you are ignorant of them. So, don't be scared. This information will help you to escape that trap. This is important, so you don't borrow money, lose it and go into debt and depression. Just be willing to work harder and carefully take all the important steps to ensure you are successful.

#1. No Quality or Serious Differentiation in the Market. Never operate a 'me too' business. When there is nothing of value that clearly differentiate your business from others, customers will not react differently. Is there anything specific and tangibly unique that you offer to your customers that your competitors are not giving them? What stands your products or service out from the crowd? Identify the ways you give advantage and tell this to the customers in the shortest and simplest language.

You must understand the importance of unique value proposition and how to clearly communicate it to your customers in a concise and compelling way. Are you faster in service delivery? Is your product superior and lower in price? If they don't know the elements that you put in to make your product or services superior, they will not react, and they will not buy.

#2. Inadequate Knowledge of Ones Line of Business. Lack of essential skills, competence, management ability and experience are the reason why 8 out of 10 new businesses fail within 5 years. Starting off without taking the time to learn what you want to do, and how to do it is preparing for failure. That you love what you do without knowing what you do makes no sense at all.

Go get experience, learn, get apprenticed however little it helps you grow fast. Warren Buffett has this to say, "Risk comes from not knowing what you are doing." Strong ability in leadership skill, sales and marketing, customer service, cash flow management, persistence, right mindset and self-belief are some of the qualities you must develop.

#3. Starting with Too Little Money. Starting with too little capital leads to failure. That is why we are showing you businesses you can start without money. If you have no money of your own, partner with people who can bring in their money for a share of the profits you will make. Be open minded, reach out, and don't let your business die in your mind.

#4. Poor Location of Business environment. Think of where your customers are and how they can come to you without stress. Consider the traffic, accessibility, packing ease. Consider location of competitors; do not put your business next door to someone who will pull all your customers. Safety of the environment and the building. Your business in a plaza is good, but people can't climb to 5th floor to get what is available on ground floor. They won't come if criminals and street urchins always hover around the environment. People won't do serious transactions in hostile environments. Your business must be suitably accessible.

#5. Over-Investment in Fixed Assets. Starting with expensive office and furniture, heavy machinery or equipment, expensive salary overhead, spending too much on advertising, engaging too many but poorly trained staff are waste most of the times especially for beginners

#6. Poor credit Arrangements. Borrowing money on 20% interest believing the business will work out. Most businesses have no record book of money flow; they don't record their expense. They are not accountable, especially when the loan is grant from government or family members. You likely fail with free money since you are not paying it back.

#7. Personal Use of Business Funds. People do not have discipline in their spending. Your business money is not for pleasure rides. Going for vacation, buying new cars. And living large too soon makes it hard for your business to survive

#8. Unexpected Growth. It is highly difficult to manage sudden successes. Even expanding too fast can lead to problems. In business you grow through experience. Ask lottery winners and people who inherited wealth what happened 12 months after. Lucky breaks without experience to manage the breakthrough leads to sudden fall from a single bad investment. Plough your profit back into your business, don't go on spending spree.

#9. Lack of Research and Testing. Inability to research and test before committing money to product, advertising or plans is bad business. Do research and survey to know what will work or what will not work. Communicate with potential buyers before investing heavily in any venture.

Valuable market research and insight can be obtained via web analytic tools. Web analytics helps you to test and know what your market audience wants to buy, what they want to know or read. It helps you to discover what is trendy among your customers. It helps you to know what activities generate traffic to your online business, so you know where to focus or invest more. Do this before you commit anything that may fail and waste your money.

#10. Inability to Withstand Competition. Fierce competition swallows businesses. Big businesses have advantages over small ones and so use strategies to drive them out of business, superior and cheaper products from big manufacturers strangle small businesses out of the market. Most small businesses have no idea how to compete with bigger or smarter people in same field.

#11. Prolonged Low Sales. If you are not making enough sales to sustain expense the business folds up. Market, advertise and get the buyers coming if you want to survive.

#12. Poor Planning. Some people think their business ideas are fantastic and will make an instant boom. Your customers determine what you do, if people are not willing to buy what you feel is fantastic you will fail big time. Test your ideas before investing in them.

#13. Choosing to do Unprofitable Business. Inability to identify and do a profitable business model that has proven revenue streams is a big problem to many people. They don't know how to think quickly and move creatively to evolve new ideas or copy innovatively what exists elsewhere. Have you seen people repairing wristwatches and umbrella? There are businesses that may generate lots of activities, but the profit potential will ensure you remain poor. Do things that are very commercially viable.

#14. Depending Solely on Your Business for Expense to Survive. Do you have reserves to sustain you before feeding your family and other living expense from a venture that has not taken off? That is why you advice people to hold on to their paid job, while they build a business by the side. Your business will crumble if you rely on it to meet all your expense when it has not stabilized.

#15. Not Determining your Customers Before Starting. The general public is not your market audience. Clearly determine who to target to patronize your product or services and research their buying habits. Not knowing the difficulty in getting people to buy, or what to do in off season when you sell a seasonal product is unwise for business.

#16. How will You Price Your Product? You must be skillful in determining your market strategy. Do you make your product cheap to sell at low prices, or do you make it the best quality and sell at a higher price? You can price yourself out of the market.

#17. Selling on Credit. If it takes customers months to pay you, your business will fail if you don't anticipate this and plan your survival ahead for it. You need cash flow to succeed.

#18. Depending on Few Great Customers. It is better to have large base small customers than depending on one big customer that will cause your business to crumble if he quits.

#19. Inability to Adapt to Changes. Market demand changes, fashion and taste changes, technology innovation causes quick changes. If you can't study your competitors to know what they are doing that you can copy, if you are not opened to new ideas your business will end abruptly.

#20. Overgeneralization. For a start, focus on one thing and inject quality and competence and excel. Spreading yourself too thin doing many things at the same time are reasons for failure. The market pays for excellence, and not for below average and poor results.

#21. Inability to Get Help from Other People. Most business owners do everything by themselves, take all the decisions and be about everything to show they are in control.

Not involving other smarter people with new and fresh ideas can lead to failures. Get advice from competent people.

#22. Inability to Plan. Most people do not plan their business effectively. It is not structured along any clear roadmap. Business is built along pattern and strategies that is well spelt out. It's not about opening your doors and selling to customers that walk in. Systemize your business.

#23. Poor Customer Service. Falling in love with your product, company, and neglecting to treat your customers with kindness is bad business. Employing untrained people who insult and annoy your clients will make sure you are out of business sooner than expected.

#24. Miscalculating Your Needs. People frequently fail to analyze the feasibility of their ideas. You fail when you miscalculate the amount required either in production, cost of borrowing, cost of meeting customer's expectations, sales or in advertising. Wrong planning leads to poor need assessments. Especially in financing. Unrealistic assumption is the reason for business failure.

#25. Unrealistic Expectations. Most people assume they will succeed immediately they open their business door. It doesn't work that way. You may have to work hard for years before your business can actually take off. And within those periods, you may have to keep putting back your profit and make serious sacrifice in tedious effort and energy.

#26. Inability to Commit. Business is real hard work and not a venture for lazy people who want to get by or get so much for doing so little. You will fail if you do not have absolute dedication and total commitment to your business. Invest time in learning new methods, try experimenting and keep developing new products, keep improving in customer services, and keep making quick decisions for your venture to grow. It's hard smart work.

#27. No Website. If you have a business today, you need a website because internet has become the new economy. Never forget that, if you don't have a website, you are most certain to keep losing business to those that have. Standard professional website makes your business look serious and good. It helps you increase revenues if you know how to leverage on its many platforms (selling ad space, generating buying traffic, drop-shipping products, or recommending affiliate products are some of the ways to make money with your website).

Every business should have a professional looking and well-designed website that enables users to easily find out about their business and how to take advantage of their products and services. Nigeria presently have 70 million people on the internet on the average during working hours. The US has over 77% of her population using the internet with nearly$ 200 billion in eCommerce sales yearly.

#28. Lack of Business Plan or Feasibility Studies Lead to Failure. Capture a concise description of your business vision, goals and target success. Access your workforce need. Analyze potential problems and possible solutions. Calculate the capital equipment, facility and infrastructures. Examine your finances in line with sales and expense forecast and cash flow. Carry out a study of possible competition will have to face. Think of marketing, advertising and promotion activities and their cost. Plan how to manage your budget and the growth of the company.

#29. Employing Incompetent Hands to Work on the Business. People give jobs to failures, relatives without skill and competences, and cheap employees who run their business down. You must engage workers smarter than you and people with skills you do not have if you must succeed.

#30. Bad Debt is Ruinous. Avoid bad debt. Borrowing is good if you invest it to yield more revenue, but borrowing for recurrent expenditure or making wrong investment with borrowed money will cause your business to crumble fast. You need to be tactical in delaying paying for loans. Ask for longer moratorium and other refinancing arrangement to delay till it is most convenient to do so. But be credit worthy, especially to banks.

#31. Employing Fraudulent Staff. Don't have crooks run any aspect of your company. Get rid of any employee the very moment you spot dishonesty in him. Monitor rigidly the activity of your employees and you too should never do anything fraudulent with your business. Pay your tax and cheat no one. A single lawsuit can wipe your business out of existence.

Chapter 4:

50 Ideas that Give You Huge Advantage as a Business Owner

#1. Don't Set Out Chasing Money, You May Never Find It: People whose ambition is primarily to make money hardly make anything meaningful, so don't go chasing money. Listen to what Bruce Barton, one of the greatest advertisers and businessmen of the 20th century said in 1928, "Money has a perverse habit of evading those who chase it too hard, and of snuggling up to folks who are partially unmindful of it".

Seek to give value to customers by offering genuine impactful services, find out how to best help, assist and render superior product or service to your customers and the money will come. The difference is in your attitude. Serve the right people genuinely and they will chase you with their money.

Still talking about money, never let lack of money stop you from doing what you want to do. True entrepreneurs never have the resources to chase their dreams. They use other people's money. Partner with people who can give you the money you need. Promise them huge profit to entice their interest to invest and finance you. It is foolish to let your dream die because you are afraid to let others come in. Never be afraid that someone will steal your ideas, even if they do, bring up more. After all, it came from your mind and no one can go there with you.

#2. Help Potential Customer to See How Your Skills Can Help Them: It is your responsibility to open the eye of your prospect to see how to help them achieve what they need that they don't know how. Most people do not know how to place a finger at what they need. They can't see it, so tell them.

Help them conceptualize it clearly and state it in the language they can understand, and they will engage you instantly.

If you understand this single reality, you will have advantage over many people. For example, most business people know that social media marketing can help their business grow, but they don't know how. If you have such experience and skill, simply approach those you believe will need your business and explain the concept to them. If they understand how they can make more money, or sell more products or services, or reach out to more people cheaper, they will engage your services. Go online, download documents to learn this skill. You don't need to go to any formal school for it. Use Google to browse all the information you need.

#3. Almost Every Business Out there is Starving for New Ideas: Don't ever forget that every business person out there is struggling to see how he can increase his sales, improve his profit or reduce his cost (of production, advertising, transportation, wages and emoluments, etc.). He is looking for how to get his staff to do more work in less time. He wants to optimize and test his processes in marketing, advertising, staff work output, the new product he wants to introduce into the market but does not know how to do these things. Your duty is to find solution to these challenges and present your ideas to him. Make him see how his business will thrive when he allows you to serve those interests.

#4. Business is All About the Customer, Not About You: This is the most important marketing rule, and you must understand it clearly if you want to make success in any endeavor. Think how best to help people solve their problems and you will be ahead of many others who are seeking opportunities where they will benefit.

The rule is don't focus on your own interest, "Sir, I can do so and so, do you have any work for me?" They will simply say, "No!" They will not give you attention. Why? Your focus and benefit are "me". Be specific about how you can solve their problem. Give value. Focus on his interest and benefit. Not your benefit. "I have an idea that will make your organization pay less tax by avoiding double taxation legitimately". "Sir, my strategy and software can help you automate your operations that will cut down your employees by half. This will save you lots of money". Your focus is benefit for him. You will get instant attention.

#5. Advertise and Make Your Product or Services Known: Most people have no way of publicizing what they do. However good you are, however great your product or service may be if people are not aware of it, then you are like someone winking in the dark. Showcase your business. There are many cheap advertising methods, platforms where you can create awareness about your business are many. Now, if your publicity or advert methods must be effective you have to take your time and learn the process. Your message, be it letter, billboard, proposal, jingle, radio or newspaper advert, flyer, whatever medium it is, your message must be very clear. You make it appealing and irresistible to the target customer reading or listening to it.

Write or talk to their level as if they are by your side listening to you. Every advert or promotional campaign must focus on what is really very important to the customer. Generously give him information about the product, enough information to realize the full benefits of your product or services to him if he should buy or consume it. If you are not able to entice him, he will not contact you or go out and buy the product. Learn about copywriting and read good books on advertising.

#6. Directly Approach People to Patronize You: Go directly to the people you target as clients or customers and approach them to buy from you or do business with you. You don't need to understand complicated marketing methods before you start. Write the approach letter and send out. Write the proposal and post it to them, they will get it and get back to you. Call them on phone and explain what you can do to improve their revenue or whatever it is you have found out that they need to become more efficient, or for their factory to run better.

Explore the social media platform to reach out and publicize what you do. Like you may know, Nigeria has the highest number of people using their telephone handset to access the internet in the whole world. That is why you see so many online shopping stores springing up and making lots of money.

Learn to connect business with your Facebook, LinkedIn, Instagram, and Twitter page. All have business usefulness built into them, people are plain ignorant about such uses. There are new and modern ways to connect businesses and effect transactions at little or no cost. Learn it. Remember, the internet gives you instant access to connect with global audience. There is nothing like it. Use it to publicize your skills and competence to reach out to people who want your services. They will contact you if you know how to do it in a way to catch their attention.

#7. Process is Very Important: In your approach letter- be it formal proposal, phone call, face to face meeting or whatever medium, don't forget to pay complement to your prospect. Clearly prove you understand your prospect's needs and challenges. Be direct, be specific and to the point, especially in establishing that you know what you are talking about.

Show your credibility and competence in explaining how you can help. Ask him to call you or write you. If you don't create a call to action, they will not know what to do after reading your mail. Specifically ask him to call you if he is interested in your proposal or whatever you are trying to sell to him. Don't stop there, do follow-up afterwards.

#8. First Research the Organization You are Trying to Approach: Besides that, people are impressed and will engage you if they know you understand their problems from the outside. Researching companies before you approach them enables you to talk to them authoritatively about the type of challenges they are having that you want to solve. Don't just make blind cold calls, it will give you very little result and you will waste a lot of time. First, do your homework well, then make the move and result will almost be guaranteed.

#9. Don't Do Business that Have Lots of Competitions: Avoid such things as general writing, fitness training, hair salon, Multi-Level Marketing for whitewashed over saturated products, computer repair and services, and such generic services that everybody is already into. You will not be noticed, you will struggle, and nobody will buy from you. That is failure already. You succeed in competitive business is you fully understand how to weave in creativity, innovation and modify (the product or service) to bring in distinctive uniqueness to create a difference from others. Don't do what others are doing, and in the same way they are doing it. Competition will strangle and kill your business. Be different in some ways.

#10. Understand the Areas Where Competition is Few: Think of problems people have. Be very specific in understanding their challenges. When you are able to identify the area where competition is few, you will have chances of commanding the market in that niche. That's where creativity, ingenuity and novelty make lots of difference. You have to be different.

The strategy is to target and build loyal customers and make them customers for life. Customers who buy your products or services and are very satisfied with it will become your loyal customers. They are more likely to buy again and again than non-customers. First, you must build trust and relationship with your customers, call them frequently, show them you care, if they have bought something from you call to know if they are enjoying the item, call to know if the machine or equipment you fixed last month is still working perfectly. Check if they have any complain, and if they do, be quick to fix it at no extra cost. When you build value and prove to be valuable to your customers they will stay with you for life.

#11. Understand How to Price Your Product or Services. There are lots of psychologies in pricing products or services. Customers associate cheap price with poor quality product, and if you charge too low for your services your client will doubt your competence. What you do is to research what other people charge for similar product or services and slightly lower your price or charges to attract customers.

The advantage you will have is if you are able to offer high quality product at a moderately reduced cost, you will pull the customers. If you sell lower priced products, you need lots of customers to make reasonable revenue. High priced products can give you higher income from few customers, but it takes longer to find such customers.

#12. Inject Uniqueness to Make the Difference: To make quick difference, you must find a way to bring uniqueness and originality into whatever you are doing. To be original you don't have to be the first, you just must be different. Being different does not mean reinventing the wheel. You creatively copy, adapt, modify and recreate what already exists. Only few people achieve originality in the true sense. Even the best of inventors steal, copy, improve and modify other people's products and ideas. They do it innovatively. Simply changing the color, fragrance, shape, taste, quantity or quality could go a long to create a difference in a competitive product you have chosen to go into.

#13. Set Your Product and Services Apart from the Pack: Don't do things like everybody else otherwise you will face overwhelming competition. Go to business premises; patiently take a study look at how others do their things. Observe what they are doing better than you, and what they are not doing well. Copy and improve on what is superior and know what advantage they lack that you can give better.

This is one of the best ways to outsmart competitors. You must be able to creatively distinguish your product, ideas or services to be successful. Never conform to what already exists and common knowledge that everybody subscribes to. The market is already overcrowded, no matter the items you are bringing into it. Set yourself apart by being more creative and outstandingly innovative even if you are selling coca cola.

#14. Seek to Distinguish Yourself in ONE Key Area. When you are special in one thing people will call you to do business with you. Always remember that you will make more money when customers are calling and running after you than when you are calling and running after them. Jack of all trade hardly makes any impact on anything.

#15. Decide the Type of Business You Want to Be Involved in. Have a clear vision of what you want. Don't just dabble into ventures you know next to nothing about simply because people are making money in it. You will end up a mediocre. Be prepared to learn fast and continuously. Be very focused once you decide what you really want to do. You must be able to answer this question in one clear precise statement, "What do you want to do?"

#16. Build Trust with Your Customers: Never deceive them to make gain. Serve their interest honestly. Give them more value for their money. Don't give or recommend product or services that are not suitable for their specific needs. Above all don't give shabby, poor, unfair and mindless services. What you think you are gaining will be lost heavily on the long run. The joy of gain from cheating others does turn sour in your mouth. Genuine business people don't mind recording loses if that is what it takes to help a customer. He knows that such a customer will be so grateful and will come back for repeat patronage; by then he will gain his money back.

#17. Deliberately Ask Referrals from Your Happy Customers: The easiest way to grow your business is through referral strategy. Develop the habit of requesting from your happy customers to introduce other people like them whom they think will need your kind of product or services. Help them to see who such people are in their life.

Maybe their relatives, friends, workmates, church members, or whoever. Promise them some reward or gift so they will be motivated to go out of their way to encourage and convince their friends to go buy from you. Remember, words of mouth marketing are the best form of advertising! Don't joke with this information if you want to make progress in your business and life endeavors.

#18. Engaging in Strategic Thinking Gives You Breakthrough Ideas: Set time apart to do strategic thinking and you will always discover breakthrough ideas to improve what you are doing. The best ideas are in your subconscious. Have the habit of deliberately taking pen and paper and turning on your creative mind and attempt to birth new ideas. You will always find something unique pouring out from your mind. Start with an hour a day, preferably early in the quiet hours of the morning, then increase the time. Do it habitually. Always act on your ideas after careful analysis. Action holds the key to all success.

#19. Read Books and Materials of Experts You Admire: Great deal of information and ideas are available, and I tell you majority of these are free online if you have access to the internet and can use your Google and YouTube. Who are the experts in your field? Who are the leaders in the industry you want to get into?

Determine these and then get their tapes, books, interviews and materials to get acquainted with the latest trends, trends in marketing and everything concerning what you are doing. Reading gives you better ideas to improve your business. Remember that the average person you see read one book in a year, imagine how far you will be ahead of them if you read one relevant book in a month.

#20. Get the Basic Tools if You Want to Do Business Online: If you want to sell online you need a website, an email list, sales page, and a product. These are the basic things you must get correctly. You can copy these ideas from people who are making progress. Remember to create and establish your uniqueness, don't just imitate blindly.

#21. Build Up Your Mental Powers: Competition is always stiff in business. If you have no idea or ability to learn faster or work smarter or build up your mental powers, you will be ordinary and ineffective. Never do a me-too kind of business. You must make a difference to excel.

#22. Study the Strategies Working Well for Others in Your Field: Spend time and money to learn and people will pay you to know what you know. Take time and study other people's business strategies. Market leaders are surely doing something special, find out what it is. Look at the technology and tools they are using. Study their packaging, observe the marketing strategies that is penetrating the market and connect them deeper with the customers and copy it.

Take a stronger look at their production and pricing mechanisms and you will learn something you can adapt into your own operations. Their ideas might help you come up with concepts you weren't thinking about. You can make more impact when you observe other businesses to identify a lapse you can fill.

#23. Know What People Really Need: To be successful you must understand what people really want and creatively offer it to them in ways no one is doing it. Courier companies came into business to relieve customer of the snail speed with which the post office delivers parcels and letters. If your document must be in another state 10am tomorrow morning, you don't go to the post office. If you satisfy customers and treat them the way other people cannot contemplate, they will become your loyal customers for life. But they may leave you if some smarter fellows tempt and pamper them with concessions and attitude more than you are giving them.

#24. Truly and Selflessly Serve People the Best Way You Can: Hire or partner with the best people to give the best to your customers. There is no negotiation when it comes to giving your customers what is needful to them. Hire experts and pay them well so they stay with you and put in their best in making your customers truly satisfied. Never cut corners by offering fake, adulterated, or poor-quality products. You will be shooting yourself on the foot. Don't ever offend, embarrass, annoy, humiliate or quarrel with your customer. He will walk away and bad mouth your business and discourage people from dealing with you. It is satisfied customers that make business grow. They will not only come for repeat patronage, they will tell others. Again, word of mouth advertising is the best advertising ever.

#25. Write Your Goals Down: Set your vision, write your goals down clearly on paper and be focused resolutely to achieving them. Don't ever leave your plans on your head. Where are you taking your business to? Where do you see your business in the next five or ten years, and what steps do you need to implement to take you there? If you have no plan, direction or destination you will be mediocre, and you can't have sufficient commitment. Your goals and objectives must include being among the best in your area. Create a vision for your business.

#26. Be Prepared to Take Risks: Most times it is the very thing you think will not work that gives surprising results and outstanding success. Never fear to dare things. Take the risk and you as well might succeed beyond your wildest imaginations. Just experiment and don't be afraid to fail.

#27. Take Whatever You Are Doing Very Seriously: You must be hungry for success before you can achieve it. Keep working very hard at what you are doing even when you are not getting results soon enough. Never do anything halfheartedly- it will fail. Never be ashamed or apologetic when you have to take your destiny into your own hands; it's your life. Those who may mock, and jeer will come around to commend when you achieve success. Shun side comments and forge ahead.

#28. Don't Depend on One Product to Succeed: Aspire to have multiple streams of passive income, but do things one after the other. If you pursue 3 rabbits at the same time, you will lose all. Beware of becoming jack of all trade in the quest to have multiple streams of income. Be strategic, but don't have just one way of getting money. The changing trends in technology, fashion, taste, vogue, etc. can wipe off within a short time, the business that was doing very well last month.

#29. Embrace Failure: Remember that people who succeed the most are the people who fail the most. Sometimes to find one breakthrough idea, you may have to work on ten that will not succeed. It is perfectly normal to fail in business. It is part of the process and nothing to be ashamed of. Just don't give up. Persevere long enough and you will win. There is no short cut. Learn from the experience of every failure and move on without being discouraged or be tempted to quit. Failure comes before success. You must be prepared to start again when you fail. Have staying power but do things with knowledge and information and it will reduce your failure rate.

#30. Go After Your Interest: People who go after their individual interest, who discover their destiny and pursue it are 100 times likely to become financially successful than those who just go after money as a priority. Remember, if you go after money, you don't find it. Simply follow your interest, work hard and work smart at developing it and money will come to you. Never lose sight of this proven truth about life and business. It is hard to be creative at jobs that do not inspire you. Do what you love and love what you do, but make sure there is commerce attached to it.

#31. The Fast-Changing World Does Not Wait for Anybody: Global trends are causing quick changes in the way businesses are done, whatever you do or where ever you do it notwithstanding. For example, selling, marketing and product advertising are all going to the internet. You have to learn the new ways of doing these things. If you don't adapt quick enough, you and your business will be wiped out. Period! Simply spend time to master the changes that is affecting your life and business and key in appropriately. Don't be left behind or allow your business to die; adapt creatively.

#32. Beware of Having a Plan B: Give all you have to the objective you have at hand. Sometimes having a plan B does not allow you to give your greatest to major thing you do. In other words, thinking of what to do when the venture at hand fails will prepare the ground for that failure. You can't give your best effort with that kind of attitude. Burn the bridge, and have the attitude of if I perish, I perish; it is either I succeed, or I perish. Take that extreme resolve, then give it your all, apply yourself completely to the business at hand. Have a single laser focus exclusively on your business plan and you will succeed.

#33. Be a Die-Hard Optimist: Stay positive and optimistic even when things are not positive. Sustain your optimism and work with undiluted enthusiasm all of the time. Be very convinced that your venture will succeed. Even if you fail, believe success is around the corner next time. Then go make one more effort. Don't forget that success comes after many failures. Many people quit too quickly and that is why they will remain failures.

#34. Be Innovation Conscious: Remember you don't have to be perfect before you start. Start and learn quickly as you go and sooner than later you will be counted as one of the professionals. Simply continue to find new ways to add more value to what you do, what you sell and how you serve your market audience or clients. Test, experiment, evaluate the impact of your product and services and watch what your competitors are doing. Let no one beat you to the game and you will be at the top. In the millennium business arena, you don't have to be big to be the best. Small companies operating with most efficient skills, technology and strategy can beat multibillion-dollar organizations hands down. Just innovate constantly.

#35. Build Your Business Around Systems: Modern business automates their business as much as possible. Your business operation is systematized if it keeps working even when you (the owner) are not there. It requires work, intelligence and knowledge. Technology has made it possible to automate most business processes especially in online business. You must build your business around systems, so you don't overwhelm yourself. Remember, an overwhelmed mind does nothing. Let your sole objective be how to deliver more value to more people in less time. To achieve this, you have to manage your time and priorities right. The best way to achieve this is to operate your business on systems.

#36. Concentrate on What You Do Best: Let your employed staff concentrate on what they do best. You should also focus on what you do best. Don't spend time doing what will give little impact. Rather, focus on the big project or tasks that are most important and not the most urgent. You must discipline yourself to concentrate on that important task that will bring in the most money.

#37. Don't Waste Time on Trivial Job Assignments: Do the planning, work out the strategies, design the process that will bring in the big money, and let your staff work out the minor details and executions. Don't be involved in washing pan, serving the customers or typing the documents. Hire people to do the time-consuming and inconsequential tasks that pay very little. You work on your business and not work in it. If you don't understand this, you will be mediocre and make little progress.

#38. Engage Experts to Perform Job Skills You Have no Competence in: Hire people to perform tasks you have no ability. Such things that are technology related require skill, and if you have not mastered it there is no point doing it. Pay someone who has the graphic design skills to work on your website. Don't do it on your own and spend the whole day and end up with a nasty result. Employ people and train them to handle serious duties that will free your time to do other creative functions. All these require hard work.

#39. To Make More Money, Serve More People: Remember, satisfied customers will always attract more customers for you. Success attracts success. In business, referrals beget referrals. So, to make more money, find new ways to serve more people more satisfactorily and they will recommend your business to their friends, colleagues, office workers, church members, club member, relatives and people with whom they have chance meeting with. Start serving well at the low level where you are and then work harder to improve. Don't forget you don't have to be 100% okay to start. But you must start to be 100% okay. Your money is in the pocket of the customers you seek. Serve them well and they will bring it out and give to you.

#40. Learn to Make Your Money Work for You: If your business start generating revenue start investing so the money will be working for you. Don't be quick to go into lavish spending and pleasure. Make your money earn more revenue in addition to the regular income from main business. The ability to delay gratification is the virtue you must learn. Be frugal, but don't live miserly or poorly. Expand your income sources so you can live a good life. That's the way to enjoy your life and not live a perpetually frugal life. The very secret many entrepreneurs and ordinary folk who seek wealth do not understand is that one becomes financially successful faster if you know how and where to put in money to make it work and earn revenue.

Salary earners earn money, spend it and wait for the next pay cheque. Like most businesses, they earn profit from their business and then blow it on things that do not add value to their business. The profits and revenue you generate must be wisely invested to earn money independent of your effort. Making money from your sweat and brows will make you grow old faster and it has lot of sufferings associated with it. Learn to compound your wealth by making your money work harder for you. It will give you rest.

#41. Embrace Good Things: Don't always reject good things that are costly or expensive but will make you happy or improve the progress of your business. Eat good food, dress well and appear like a successful person all the time. If you project the impression of success, people will assume you are one and treat you well. There is nothing wrong about using costly materials or resources that help build your business or add value to your life. What is wrong is paying expensive price for a material you can get much cheaper elsewhere.

A good businessman knows what to buy, where to get the best price, and he doesn't throw his money away to prove he has the ability to pay. Know the difference. You must be a good representative of your company. Pay your workers well, if not, they will leave you to work for someone who can pay better. Don't be stingy, miserly, selfish or greedy, you will lose.

#42. Don't Be Involved in Ventures No One is Willing to Pay for: Quickly get out of any business that is not making money for you or does not have the capacity to make much money, no matter how much passion you have for it. If you do the kind of business that people are reluctant to pay for you will be poor. The alternative is to do the business and have another business that will make you money by the side. Know the activities that are waste of time. You must know how to put your activities to profitable use. Passion cannot be sustained on an empty pocket. Do businesses that have proven to attract lots of buyers. Competitive business is good because it is a proof people are interested in the product or service.

#43. People will Always Pay You to Solve their Problems: You don't have to be the best to make money (if you are it helps anyway). All you need to do is to be better than those people who want your help in solving their problems. People will always pay when you have the solution they are looking for. To be the solution provider, you must have the know-how.

#44. Online Business: Lots of business opportunities exist online. Digital technology gives you an easier way to create your own job and make money. Nigeria has the highest number of people using their mobile telephone handset to access the internet. That is why most online shopping sites are making lots of money now. Begin to think how you can leverage on the craze of online business; know that 6 out of 10 richest people in the world operate through technology.

You just must approach it with knowledge and determination. It is all learnable and you don't need to be a tech savvy person to do it. For example, if you want more online sales, there are two basic ways to do it. You either get more traffic or get a higher conversion of people visiting your website. The knowledge takes a study and interest, but the possibility is real, as a matter of fact, the internet is the economy of the new millennium. The dynamics of what works is always changing. Strategies that brought massive results yesterday may fail woefully tomorrow.

#45. Be an Unending Learner: There is no alternative to learning. Ignorance is the number one reason for mediocrity and failure. You can't pretend to know what you do not know in business. The result will always show because it is hard to fake competence for long. So, keep learning new methods, new things, new strategies; keep discovering and using new tools, especially technology tools that make the process easier, faster, automated and systematized. You must keep updating your knowledge to keep abreast with developments, trends and events in your business fields.

#46. If You Can't Pull through Your Ideas Cooperate, Partner and Collaborate with Others: If you have great ideas but can't sell or market, then it is wiser to partner with someone who can market it, and split the proceeds from such transaction with them on agreed terms. You are tech savvy but marketing shy. All you need do is get a partner who can go to the prospects and pull out the deal. Do the job and share the money with the partner.

The essence of business is to partner with someone who can complement your deficiencies. Most people allow their money-spinning ideas to die for lack of money or skill. That shows poor thinking. Don't develop a plan that will take tons of cash to start, even when you find the capital to fund it. Failure will make you and your investors lose heavily. Start small and grow bigger gradually.

#47. Become Financially Literate: Do you have the habit of paying yourself first each time any money comes into your hands- no matter the pressure of debt or insufficiency of the amount? That is, you remove at least 10% of that money and save, accumulate and then invest it in a venture where the money will be working and earning more money for you? Do you have discipline in spending and handling money? Can you afford not to tell anyone when huge amount of money comes to you? Can you resist lending, buying things on impulse, becoming emotional in decisions, giving out the money to friends and relatives, and spending your financial windfalls for at least six months?

It is expected of a business person to read numbers and understand figures and do little arithmetic. But that is not the matter here. Get financial literacy that will help you take good charge of your business. Business requires some knowledge of simple mathematics. Knowing how to take control of your money and making wise investment are some of the sure ways to guarantee success in business. Financial intelligence- which is information, wisdom, knowhow, and knowledge regarding money affairs go a long way to determine failure or success, or whether you will be rich or poor. You must be financially literate. Invest in this information compulsorily.

#48. Please, Learn the Rules of Wealth: Money has rules, I mean new rules! The rules that profitably multiply your money. The art of channeling your money and investments properly to work for you. It is the knowledge you have about your business or money that makes you successful. Hard work alone does not make anybody successful. Work hard with the right knowledge and relevant information. You need to know the rules of profitable investing, so you don't accumulate money after years of hard work, then waste it on unwise and foolish investments based on poor decisions. It could be painful. Talk to retirees who took their money, invest it in one or two business ventures and are broke eight months after.

#49. Entrepreneurs Have More Chances of Becoming Financially Successful than Salary Earners: If you want to make money then go do business. This is a fact; doing business and becoming an entrepreneur, working for yourself gives you more chances of making success and becoming rich with guaranteed future.

Most job condition and terms of employment forbids you from doing any other business. With the unpredictable nature of today's economy, no job security exists anywhere. Your employment can be terminated anytime and for any reason. Your livelihood and the fate of your family exist at the pleasure of some other fellows when you work for them. Business allows you to be at the driving seat of your life. Those who value paid employment hardly think of learning what it takes to solve problems. Doing routine job assignments do not give you enough experience to solve people's or organizational problems. Most employees are poor and mostly losers with no initiative.

#50. Ask this Question: "What will my destiny become if I choose to create my chance and take my destiny in my hands to direct my financial future by myself?" If you find a good answer to this question, then you will think of becoming not just an entrepreneur, but a successful one who creates employment for others. It is something you can learn, and you can do it. The nation and indeed nations are looking for such people for they are real nation builders. Be one!

Please, I Need Your Feedback

"Hey there! If you enjoyed this book, I'm guessing you'll probably love my other books. Sign up for the free newsletter to get special deals and hear about all my newest books before anyone else. You can get on the list here:

List of Books Written by Ucheka Anofienem

Business Books

#1. 177 Lucrative Businesses You Can Start without Money

#2. Unique Ideas to Pamper Your Customers So They Keep Coming Back to Buy and Advertise You to Others

#3. Why Salary Earners Are Losers

#4. 1000 Methods to Attract Customers to Your Business Place

#5. Fastest Ways to Win Many Customers and Clients without Spending Much Money

#6. Creative Ways to Manage Small Business Loan to Grow Your Business and Pay Back Fast

#7. Creative Ideas to Attract All the Customers from Your Competitors

#8. Modern Marketer's Tools: Skills and Qualities that Wao Customers and Get the Money

#9. Free Money to Fund You're your Business Ideas

#10. Are You Making these 33 Terrible Mistakes that Cause New Businesses to Fail Quickly?

#11. Small Agricultural Businesses that Can Make You Too Much Money

#12. Agricultural Value Chain and How You Can Profit from Government's Agro Entrepreneurial Drive

#13. Quick Action Ideas for Making Money

#14. Creative Strategies to Re-Awaken a Hotel Business

#15. Existing Advert Space Potentials that Can Earn Tons of Cash for You- for Free

#16. Travel Agency Marketing Strategies

#17. Fastest and Most Effective Way to Sell Landed Properties

Quote Books

#18. Most Valuable Instructions for Living the Best Life: Counsel of Wise Men from the Ancient

#19. Words in Apple of Pure Gold: Ancient Life-Transforming Immortal Truth As You Have Never Heard It Before

#20. Captivating Money Quotes that Make You Richer, Wiser, and Happier

#21. Best Business Growth Advice from World's Greatest Entrepreneurs

#22. How You Attract What Happens in Your Life: The Exact Words of those That Know Precisely

#23. How to Serve Your Customers to Keep Buying Only from You, Bring their Friends and Publicize You for the Rest of their Lives

#24. Sales and Marketing Wisdom that Helps You Sell Like Magic

#25. Inspirational Proverbs that Make You Wiser than Solomon

#26. Sweetest Chinese Wisdom

Self-Development Books

#27. Greatest Unusual Secrets to Live By: Using Contrary Wisdom to Achieve Super Success and Fulfilment

#28. How to Discover Your Natural Talents

#29. Rising to Great Heights

#30. Habits that Make You A Special Personality

#31. Super Charisma: Ideas to Become An Extraordinary Person at An Instant

#32. How to Make People Like You

#33. Lifestyles that Make You Happy All Day

#34. Fastest Way to Secure Your Dream Job Today, Even without Vacancy

#35. What Every Unemployed, Underemployed and Employer Should Know

#36. Office Etiquettes that Guarantee Productivity and Safety

#37. How to Profit from Your Obstacles, Hard Times and Adversities

#38. How to Avoid Digging Your Grave with Your Lifestyle

#39. Creative Thoughts for Higher Life

#40. Nice Guy and Ideal Lady: 1000 Ideas to Be Most Recognized Among Your Peers

#41. People Who Have these Qualities Have Everything in Life.

Christian and Spiritual Books

#42. Rich and Miserable: the Agony of Faulty Wealth

#43. The Miraculous Power of Giving

#44. Your Mouth Can Kill, Even You

#45. Equipped for Victory

#46. Salvation to Fulfil Your Divine Destiny

#47. Christian Pilgrim's Guide to Holy Land: How to Safely Navigate Your Way in Israel and Totally Enjoy Your Journey and Visits While there

General Interest Books

#48. Nigerian Mentality: The Real Trouble with Nigerians

#49. Who Are the Bombastic Elements?

Relationship Books

#50. How to Find Sweet Someone to Marry You in 3 Months

Humor Book

#51. Humors that Make You Quake with Laughter

Children Books

#52. Character Building and Moral Education for Children and Young Adults

#53. Things that Belong to Me As A Child

#54. Safety Guide for Children and Young Adults

#55. Strange Village and Other Stories for Children

Literary Books (Drama Texts)

#56. The Stigmatized

#57. The Innocent Victims

#58. Liberation for Almajiri

#59. Child Survival

#60. No More Stolen Mandates

Collection of Poems

#61. Decadent Purity

School Educational Materials

#62. Study Skills for Excellent Grade Improvement

#63. Teachers Guide for Improved Grade Performance

#64. Security Education, Common Crimes and Security Management 1. For Junior Secondary Schools (JSS) 1

#65. Security Education, Common Crimes and Security Management 11. For Junior Secondary Schools (JSS) 2

#66. Security Education, Common Crimes and Security Management 111. For Junior Secondary Schools (JSS) 3

#67. Security Education: Concept of Security for Primary 1

#68. Security Education: Sources of Danger and Insecurity for Primary 2

#69. Security Education: Elements of Criminal Behavior for Primary 3

Security Conscious Books

#70. Basic Security Awareness for Your Safety

#71. Corp Member's Comprehensive Security Handbook

#72. Essential Information and Awareness for Nigerian Peace Corps Members

#73. Survival and Safety Guide for Technical Aid Corps Volunteers

#74. Safety Tips for Visitors and Travelers in Nigeria

#75. New Professional Behavior, Etiquettes and Modern Standards in Nigerian Police

#76. Professional Behavior, Social Rules and New Standards in Nigerian Security and Civil Defense Corps

#77. Modern Etiquettes, Values and New Standards in Nigerian Military

Politics

#78. Women! Go Take Your Place in Leadership Now!

#79. New Ways Women Can Win Elections

#80. More Women in Government

Book

Images

177 Lucrative Businesses You Can Start without Money. $44.97c

Small Agricultural Businesses that Can Make You Too Much Money. $19.97c

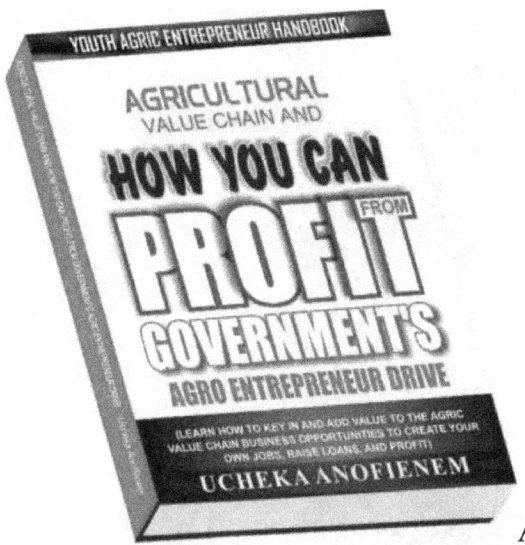

AGRICULTURAL VALUE CHAIN and How You Can Profit from Government's Agro Entrepreneur Drive. $ 19.97c

Best Business Growth Advice from World's Greatest Entrepreneurs. $22.47c

Free Money to Fund Your Business Ideas. $19.97c

Unique Ideas to Pamper Your Customers So They Keep Coming Back to Buy and Advertize You to their Friends. $ 22.47c

Fastest Ways to Win Many Customers & Clients without Spending Much Money. $27.97c

Fastest Way to Secure Your Dream Job Today. Even without Vacancy. $15.47c

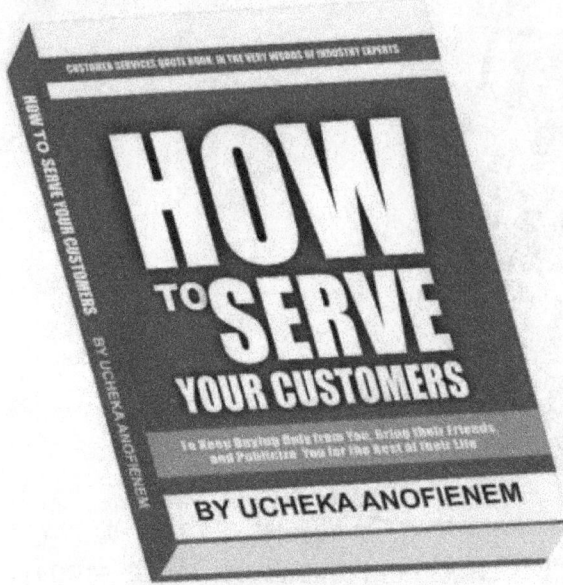

How to Serve Your Customers. $16.97c

Greatest Unusual Secrets to Live By: Using Contrary Wisdom to Achieve Super Success and Fulfilment. $47.79C

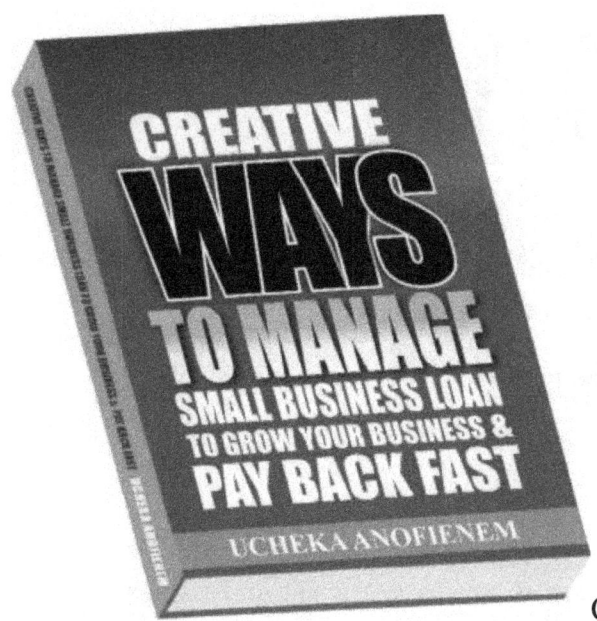

Creative Ways to Manage Small Business Loan to Grow Your Business & Pay Back Fast. $19.47c

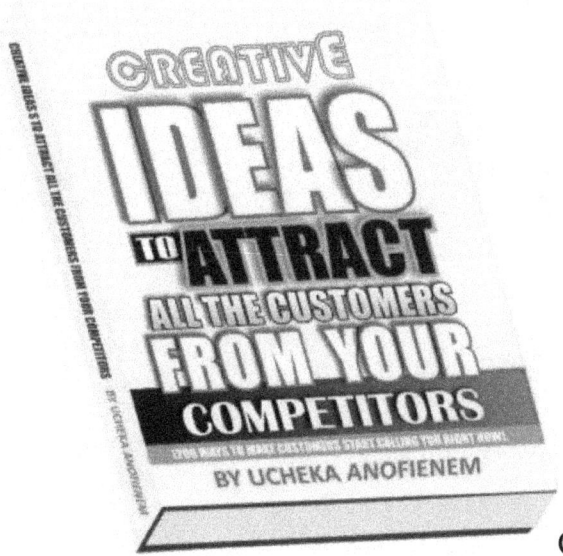

Creative Ways to Manage Small Business Loan to Grow Your Business & Pay Back Fast. $19.47c

Creative Ways to Manage Small Business Loan to Grow Your Business & Pay Back Fast. $19.47c

Are You Making these 50 Terrible Mistakes that Cause New Businesses to Fail Quickly? $39.47c

Hire Ucheka

Ucheka Anofienem is a highly sought-after value-oriented business development strategist, an innovative marketer and impactful career trainer. You have a chance to work with him one-on-one to build your business or start-up one. He has authored too many excellent business and self-development books including the best-selling 177 Lucrative Businesses You Can Start without Money, Creative Ideas to Attract All the Customers from Your Competitors, Why Salary Earners Are Losers, Best Business Advice from World Greatest Entrepreneurs, and over 40 other books- too many to list here.

Ucheka is skilled in knowledge and information transfer, and a delight as keynote speaker in seminars, conference and workshops. He is an excellent teacher that gives much more value for money paid. Since you are now ready to advance your business to higher levels, hire Ucheka if you need concrete money spinning, cost saving ideas to move your business to higher levels. He is a renowned marketing strategist, and best-selling author, Email: ucheka1968@gmail.com, **Tel: 234(0)8164746117.** We guarantee to meet your very needs and excel your expectations.

Speaking Engagements with Ucheka

An inspiring, motivational, entertaining and highly engaging speaker. Always poised to give undiluted value and massive influence that get listeners reeling with satisfaction and looking forward for more! He is noted for motivating people to take massive upscaling action to set and attain goals.

Focused On:

Customer Acquisition, Innovative Business Development Strategies, Life-Transforming Success Habits, Creative and Innovative Marketing, Concept Development Writing, Workforce Capacity Building, and Book Writing Skills. Ucheka superbly delivers creative messages.

Businesses, companies and clients whose objectives are to outsell, overtake, excel, outthink, outclass, outperform, out strategize, out market, gain market competitors, gain dominance in market share advantage, engage our services.

If you want to understand all that's possible for your business-especially in identifying how to tap hidden and overlooked opportunities, build leveraging relationships, and adopt unusual approaches to outperform your competitors, then talk to us. **Call 234(0)8164746117. Email:** ucheka1968@gmail.com**, Tel: 234(0)8164746117.** We will work with you personally and directly to get things done. We have materials and books you can take immediate advantage of and have more specifically developed to suit your peculiar needs or circumstances.

For Cost of Booking and Engagements- both locally and internationally, place a call for details. Email: ucheka1968@gmail.com, **Tel: 234(0)8164746117**

Ucheka gives undivided attention and commits to deeply listen to understand your real needs and proffer uncommon solution that gives you more than desired results.

What Do You Really Need That We Can Serve to Meet?

Competition and Customer Concerns, Marketing Strategy Challenges? Business Winning Sale Letter, Marketing and operational Critique, Career and Business Growth Consulting, Social Media Campaign, Speaking at Your Events, Youth Empowerments and Skill Impartation Workshops? Email and Ad Copy Writing? Content Developments? Document Developments?

Just call: Tel:234 (0)8164746117, Email: Ucheka1968@gmail.com

About the Book

It is very possible to do business and render services to people without money. I mean no money at all. The sense and creativity you need, and those very services that will help you to earn money right from day one is what this book will show you. Be ready to discover what you have not been thinking about before now and get ready to employ yourself or extend your efficiency after reading this book.

This is simple. Concentrate on mobile services. Meet people where they are and serve them directly with your initiative, skills, competence and experience. This book points out products and services that will not require renting shops, office space, buying big equipment, or paying monthly bills. Forget about capital intensive businesses. Just have the willingness to move yourself to act now. All the ideas you need are here. Just read on.

About the Author

Ucheka Anofienem- Director, Skill Development Information System Ltd. Ucheka helps business owners and organizations to expand their capacity to make money by using overlooked marketing and leveraging strategies. An Idea Creator; Breakthrough Thinker; Human Capital; and Business Development consultant.

Since 1998, he has worked to create capacity building value for organizations and clients. Ucheka is a Document Development Specialist, Research Writer, Business Coach, and Author with over ten published works. His first degree is in English and Literature, Master's degree in International Law and Diplomacy from the Universities of Benin and Jos respectively. Contact: 234 (0) 8164746117, 08098610247Email: ucheka1968@gmail.com